Praise for *Filthy Shakespeare*:

"This jaw-dropping, giggle-inducing text proves both the Bard's enduring relevance and the fact that today's most popular entertainment isn't nearly as debased as some might think."                    —*Publishers Weekly*

"A romp of a read."                    —*The Associated Press*

"Brush up on your Shakespeare from a bawdy angle . . . amusing . . . will intrigue Bard lovers."                    —*Encore Magazine*

"If you think the directive 'sex sells' is unique to this modern age of bra-baring starlets and orgasm-mimicking shampoo commercials, you might want to brush up on your sixteenth-century Elizabethan literature. . . . *Filthy Shakespeare* will definitely change the way you remember the 'romantic' dialogue between Romeo and Juliet."                    —*Nylon* magazine

"Brilliant."                    —*Philadelphia Weekly*

"A great gift for anyone who loves Shakespeare."                    —*British Weekly*

"Goes some way towards wiping out that sneaking feeling you often get reading the Bard's sublime verse that you're not quite in on the joke . . . fascinating."                    —*The Guardian*

"Great fun."                    —*The Times Literary Supplement* (London)

"A beautifully presented guide to Elizabethan filth."                    —*The Observer*

STUDIO 8

Dr. Pauline Kiernan holds a doctorate from the University of Oxford, where she taught for many years, and is the author of the acclaimed *Shakespeare's Theory of Drama* (Cambridge University Press). She was appointed Leverhulme Research Fellow to work on productions at the new Globe on Bankside in its first years. Her scholarship on Shakespeare and Renaissance Drama has captivated worldwide audiences. She lives in England.

# FILTHY
# SHAKESPEARE

## Shakespeare's Most Outrageous Sexual Puns

### PAULINE KIERNAN

GOTHAM BOOKS

GOTHAM BOOKS
Published by Penguin Group (USA) Inc.
375 Hudson Street, New York, New York 10014, U.S.A.

Penguin Group (Canada), 90 Eglinton Avenue East, Suite 700, Toronto, Ontario, M4P 2Y3,
Canada (a division of Pearson Penguin Canada Inc.); Penguin Books Ltd, 80 Strand, London
WC2R 0RL, England; Penguin Ireland, 25 St Stephen's Green, Dublin 2, Ireland
(a division of Penguin Books Ltd); Penguin Group (Australia), 250 Camberwell Road,
Camberwell, Victoria 3124, Australia (a division of Pearson Australia Group Pty Ltd);
Penguin Books India Pvt Ltd, 11 Community Centre, Panchsheel Park, New Delhi - 110 017,
India; Penguin Group (NZ), 67 Apollo Drive, Rosedale, North Shore 0632, New Zealand
(a division of Pearson New Zealand Ltd.); Penguin Books (South Africa) (Pty) Ltd,
24 Sturdee Avenue, Rosebank, Johannesburg 2196, South Africa

Penguin Books Ltd, Registered Offices: 80 Strand, London WC2R 0RL, England

Published by Gotham Books, a member of Penguin Group (USA) Inc.

Previously published in Great Britain in 2006 by Quercus and
in 2007 as a Gotham Books hardcover edition

First trade paperback printing, October 2008
9  10

Gotham Books and the skyscraper logo are trademarks of Penguin Group (USA) Inc.

Copyright © 2006 by Pauline Kiernan
All rights reserved

ISBN 978-1-592-40401-8

Printed in the United States of America

While the author has made every effort to provide accurate telephone numbers and Internet
addresses at the time of publication, neither the publisher nor the author assumes any
responsibility for errors, or for changes that occur after publication. Further, the publisher
does not have any control over and does not assume any responsibility for author
or third-party Web sites or their content.

For my sister Patricia

# CONTENTS

# ACKNOWLEDGEMENTS

The first person I must thank is Shakespeare himself. Being in his company for so many years of my life is an experience hard to sum up. That a single individual knew so much about the human condition never ceases to take my breath away.

I would like to thank my former Shakespeare students at Oxford for their enthusiasm and inspiration; and my publisher and editor at Quercus, Richard Milbank, for his spirited and exuberant support for the idea for the book, as well as his diligent editing. Needless to say, any errors that remain are mine. I would also like to thank Two Associates, the designers of the book, for making it look so elegant; to say a big thank you to my agent, Susan Smith; and also to record a special debt of gratitude to the author Julie Summers for her nagging me to go ahead and write a book that has been bubbling away in my head for so many years.

I want to say a very special thank you to Colin Robson for many years of support and encouragement, and for our endless discussions about Shakespeare, and to our son Michael who made sure my sense of humour stayed intact throughout the writing of this book. He also copy-read the manuscript like a true professional.

The dedication reflects my long-held gratitude to my big sister, Patricia, who, needing an audience for rehearsing a speech for a school recital, introduced a wide-eyed five-year-old to the strange, wondrous-sounding language of a ham omelette mysteriously troubled by a bee.

# A NOTE BEFORE YOU BEGIN

Shakespeare must have been mercilessly ribbed all his life. He was a walking, talking, breathing sexual pun. In fact, he was a double-sexual pun. His name meant Wanker – to shake one's spear. So much for his surname. His Christian name was a pun on prick, cunt and sexual desire.

Will Shakespeare was called a Prick Wanker. Or A Wanker On Cunts. Or a sexually aroused Wanker. Even if you substitute the slang for more polite expressions, he's still a Penis Masturbator, or Penis Shaker.

But without the sexual puns, both his names suggest strength of will and determination. So, although many of the following examples of his sexual punning cloak the ribald meanings and significances of a word, it doesn't necessarily mean that the subtext cancels out the surface meaning.

Will Shakespeare, then, meant a Prick Wanker. But the names also meant someone strong and courageous. And with this particular Will Shakespeare, they stood for someone unafraid to shake others out of their complacent assumptions about sexual identity, politics, war, and morality.

# INTRODUCTION

## Sex in Shakespeare's time

# PIMPS, WHORES AND
# A SWOLLEN PRICK

round the corner from the Globe Theatre where Shakespeare's
most famous plays were performed was a brothel, one among
untold numbers that lined London's Bankside in those days
(bank – brothel district). It was one of the more sophisticated knocking-
shops and it was called 'The Cardinal's Hat', named for the colour of the
tip of an engorged penis.

Everyone, of course, knew why it was called what it was, just as they
would have known that 'tongue' was something in the mouth used for
speaking, but could also mean a woman's clitoris; that 'noon' was the
name for midday but also for the erect penis at its height (as in pointing
up to twelve on a dial); and that if you called someone 'slippery', you were
most likely describing a bisexual.

It is quite amazing how little attention has been given to
Shakespeare's vulgar, lewd, downright filthy puns. His plays and poems
are stuffed with the kind of double entendres and obscene wordplay that
would make our most risqué stand-up comics blush. Puns on cunt,
sodomy, VD, masturbation, semen, same-sex fucking, male whores,
female whores, impotence – you can find all of them in nearly every play.

# THE TANTALISING SUBTEXT

hakespeare's audiences were fine-tuned to hearing what we now
call subtext in a way that we can hardly begin to imagine. When
they talked of going to the theatre they called it going to hear a
play, not to see one. In the playhouses, open to the skies, with
performances in daylight, with nothing like our elaborate set design and
lighting to create mood, establish location, and provide visual signals for
the audience to follow, listening closely to the words was essential.

At the Globe, the actor was surrounded by three thousand spectators,
or six thousand listening ears. And those ears were trained to hear every
nuance of meaning in a word, including, and especially, ones with sexual

undertones. This was because so many people used language in this way and because, quite simply, they went to so many plays. Two hundred of them every season, different plays performed six days each week, with one in eight Londoners going to them every week, many going twice or three times a week. And with each theatre holding up to three thousand playgoers at a time, it is little wonder Shakespeare's audiences were such skilled listeners and could decode a sexual pun instantaneously.

# LONDON - A THEATRE OF PUNISHMENT, GREED AND DISEASE

But there is another reason why the audiences of the time were habituated to the language of the street, and it lies in just that: the street. It is important to remember when exploring Shakespeare's obscene puns that he inhabited a world that can, to us, seem indecent, vulgar, and brutal. People spoke a language that was full of figures of speech – bawdy, colourful, or just plain gross – to describe or disguise the cruel facts of life: poverty, the plague, venereal disease, a high infant mortality rate, slow painful death, the brutal violence in many forms that was everywhere around them.

Life in Shakespeare's England was – for many of its population – brutal, hard and raw. Mass unemployment in the country as a whole, combined with failed harvests which forced the price of grain up 400 per cent, meant that thousands were starving to death. Shakespeare's last tragedy, *Coriolanus*, actually opens on a scene of hungry protesters wielding weapons and demonstrating against the famine the authorities have created by the hoarding of corn to push prices up. There were popular uprisings like this throughout the country, including one in Shakespeare's home county of Warwickshire, at the time he was writing this play.

The number of homeless increased every day – they drifted from town to town, sleeping rough, begging. A quarter of London's population was lost to the plague in 1563, the year before Shakespeare was born.

In 1593, when eleven thousand people died of the plague the playwright would have walked streets where the stench of putrefied corpses piled up was as horrific as the sight of the black skin stretched over skeletal bodies, rats and maggots eating their eyes, beetles and flies nesting in their open mouths behind blue, blotched lips. When he lived north of the river, he would have had to walk to work through the appalling squalor of the town ditch and passed the pitiful chained inmates of the mental asylum, Bedlam, who provided unwanted entertainment and amusement to sightseers.

As well as the theatres, there was another spectacle Londoners flocked to. Punishment of crime was made ghoulishly public. Traitors would be strung up till only half dead, have their bowels ripped out, their legs hacked off, and their head sliced from their bodies. Or you could watch traitors tied to a stake and see their bodies licked by flames, a human bonfire, slowly burning to death. Almost every day, you would have been able to watch a form of public execution at one of several London sites. Gruesome rituals and violent death figure again and again in Shakespeare, and often the language which describes them is a grotesque form of sexual wordplay.

These were the realities of a world where life was a daily battle against starvation and disease and above all, by our standards, short. The average life expectancy for men has been estimated as 30–35 in wealthy London districts and 20–25 in the poorer parts, although some people did live on into their 50s. Between 30 and 40 per cent of the country's population were poor, and the gap between rich and poor grew wider during Shakespeare's lifetime.

It was also the time of rising capitalism, of the creation of the middle classes, growing rich and powerful – often through questionable business practices – and of an attitude of every man for himself. Shakespeare's *Timon of Athens* shows a world where luxury goods pouring into the ports from all corners of the earth were prompting greed on an unprecedented level. And with greed, came credit – borrowing vast sums to maintain an extravagant lifestyle. Pawnbrokers and loan sharks – the equivalent of our banks today who charge us exorbitant interest – were always kept busy. It may please some of us today to learn that Shakespeare's contemporaries called bankers financial prostitutes. The court of

Elizabeth I was a byword for depravity, with aristocrats ruthlessly jostling for power and for the lucrative monopolies on luxury goods.

Greed for money is often likened to lust and sexual perversion in Shakespeare. The upwardly mobile desire of the self-loving servant Malvolio in *Twelfth Night* is characterised in terms of sex, and gives rise (if you'll forgive the pun) to one of the most uproarious examples of Shakespeare's play on the word 'cunt' (see page 61).

## FAECES, FLATULENCE AND FESTERING POX

hakespeare's London cannot begin to be imagined without feeling it on the senses. The city was bursting at the seams, its population exploding from 200,000 in 1574 to 400,000 in 1642. The assaults on the sense of smell and of hearing were ferocious. The bellowing of hawkers and the clatter of traffic competed with the bells of 114 churches ringing out every hour, day and night.

And the smell. The Thames itself a fetid sewer that was also London's water supply, the streets and thoroughfares used for evacuating bowels and bladders, the belching, putrid smoke from factories (the hazelnuts found at the site of the Rose and Globe theatres were waste products from a nearby soap factory), everything conspired to make the battle against disease and bubonic plague an impossible one. The 1593 epidemic closed the theatres and led to the banning of all public gatherings. It's little wonder the plays of the time are full of references and puns on faeces, and flatulence and bodies encrusted with festering, putrid plague and boils. Venereal disease was rife, and Shakespeare frequently alludes to the plague to talk about that other disease and those other boils – of the pox.

# WHORES, WHEELER-DEALERS AND PICKPOCKETS IN THE HOUSE OF GOD

In the old St Paul's Cathedral across the Thames, opposite the Globe, hundreds of English and foreign merchants from the great trading countries of the world crammed the aisles, wheeling and dealing, using the marble tombs and even the baptismal font for counting out money, to the sound of the divine services being sung by the Cathedral choir. Punters picked up prostitutes, male as well as female, lawyers made deals, pickpockets picked pockets, while others came to look at the small ads posted on the walls, for jobs, services, and language lessons – Arabic, French, Russian, Polish and Dutch were in great demand as more and more people wanted to find out about those foreign lands whose tall three-masted ships unloaded their cargoes at the crowded wharves and warehouses of London's dockland.

St Paul's was also an extraordinary bazaar, lined with shops on two levels – you could pick up your groceries on the way out and then browse among the many bookstalls that were set out in the courtyard, and buy a quarto copy of a Shakespeare play.

# THE BISHOP'S TARTS

The theatres themselves were built in the district of the whore-houses and Molly-houses (male brothels) on the south bank of the Thames, which were licensed by the Bishop of Winchester who made a fortune from them and who was satirised by Shakespeare for his hypocrisy of growing fat on the sins of the flesh. The Southwark whores were known as 'Winchester geese', and the sound of the word 'geese' was the hiss or wheeze that VD sufferers made. In these brothels there would be 'all the equipments needed by sadists and masochists, with the necessary female (or, if need be, male) partners'.

People called the brothels 'stews', named after the vapour baths customers sweated through in the hope of steaming venereal disease from their bodies.

Bankside was the site of London's sex industry which Shakespeare most famously recreates in his plays – the brothel madam called Mistress Quickly (Quick-Lay/Quick-Fuck) who appears in three History plays and a comedy is one of Shakespeare's most sparkling characters. More disturbingly, in *Measure for Measure* the whole plot revolves around ridding the city of its pimps and whorehouses by a Puritan deputy ruler who is seized with lust and tries to blackmail a novice nun into having sex with him. Bankside was London's underworld, outside the jurisdiction of the Lord Mayor and the Puritans, a place where criminals operated, and the convicted were thrown into one of its five prisons.

East along the river was the Tower of London. Here, coming from the theatre having watched one of Shakespeare's most gruesome, violent scenes, playgoers could witness another spectacle: a political prisoner mounting the scaffold and having his head chopped off, stuck on a pike, and displayed on London Bridge. One foreign tourist counted 34 such heads. (Shakespeare himself has the severed heads of Macbeth and Richard III brought on stage, moments which would have been a lot less chilling for his original audiences than they are for us.)

London Bridge was the only bridge over the Thames. Lined with houses and shops, and clogged with a permanent traffic jam, it was a sight that all tourists of the time came to see. 'The most beautiful bridge in the world,' one French visitor called it. A playwright of that time wrote that 'in every street carts and coaches make such a thundering as if the world ran on wheels'. Bankside was always packed too – some 4000 people crossed the river by boat every day to visit the theatres. And who knows how many more made the crossing using London's 2000 wherries (river taxis), to buy sex, watch the grisly spectacle of bear-baiting, or to pick pockets. This mass of heaving humanity would jostle against one another in the streets and alleys of Bankside – what was aptly called 'the margins' of society.

It was here that Philip Henslowe, famous theatre impresario, money lender, property speculator and brothel-owner, took out a lease on a whorehouse called The Rose (rose – vagina and brothel). When he built a new theatre on the site he probably kept the brothel going as well. The wife of the actor Edward Alleyn, one of the two A-list celebrities of the day (the other was Shakespeare's chief actor, Dick Burbage), was probably a brothel madam there. For her sins she was drawn through the streets of Southwark, like many prostitutes, in an open cart – this being the shaming ritual for captured whores. At the time, theatres were viewed as no better than the brothels and bear pits. They were lumped together with all manner of lewd and grotesque entertainments.

# SHAKESPEARE'S ARISTOCRATIC PATRON GETS A PAINFUL DOSE

It was not just bishops and theatrical entrepreneurs who dealt in the flesh trade. Queen Elizabeth I gave her Lord Chamberlain, who was the patron of Shakespeare's acting company, the licences for brothels in the area of Paris Garden not far from the Rose. The aristocratic patron, then, of Shakespeare's company, grew rich from prostitution (as well as property speculation), but he also, unfortunately, grew painfully ill with venereal disease, and was known to subject himself to the agonising mercury treatment believed at that time to alleviate syphilis. It is also worth mentioning that Chamberlain was renowned for his foul mouth. A contemporary wrote of 'his custom of swearing, and obscenity in speaking'. He had ten known illegitimate children, one of whom became the Bishop of Exeter. His venereal disease does not seem to have put a stop to his sex life – it is believed he fathered a daughter at the age of 70. There was another public figure known for the coarseness of his language: Queen Elizabeth's successor, James I, was known for being a foul-mouthed king.

# COVERT SODOMITES AND 'LASCIVIOUS WRITHINGS OF TENDER LIMBS'

A whore cost less than going to a play or the bear pit – where you could watch half a dozen mastiffs let loose on and rip apart a bear tied to a stake. The theatres were the subject of outraged condemnation by the Puritans and other 'anti-theatricals', one of whom, Phillip Stubbes, ranted:

> *'Mark the flocking and running to the theatres . . . daily and hourly, night and day, time and tide, to see plays and interludes, where such wanton gestures, such bawdy speeches, such kissing and glancing of wanton eyes and the like is used . . . Then these pageants being done, every mate sorts to his mate, every one brings another homeward of their way very friendly, and in their secret conclaves covertly play the Sodomites or worse.'*

Reading such diatribes, it's tempting to imagine such men watching plays, working themselves up to a fever pitch of fear of contamination, a veritable froth of sexual frenzy, terrified of being aroused by such a disturbing contamination, that their condemnation feels like an ejaculation of rage against the 'Evil Temptress' – The Theatre! All the 'anti-theatricals' of the time comment on the sexually provocative nature of plays and playgoing.

There were no women actors at the time, the female parts being played by boy-actors or 'play-boys', as they were called. One poor man unwittingly damns himself with a particularly sexy description of what he's supposed to be denouncing. He has clearly been aroused by what he describes as 'the lascivious writhings of their tender limbs and gorgeous apparel'. You can almost hear the heavy breathing.

# HOMOSEXUAL
# AND LESBIAN DESIRE

ociety in Shakespeare's time did not divide sexuality into heterosexual and homosexual as we do today. No one then would have actually called themselves 'a homosexual'. That's because the sexuality of the individual was not the starting- point for defining personal identity. The Elizabethans acknowledged that same-sex desire existed, and the literature and the visual arts of the period offered many examples of homoerotic and lesbian desire. But the whole subject was highly blurred and full of inconsistencies.

The word 'sodomy', for example, was a catch-all term that covered anal penetration by a penis, a finger, a dildo or other object involving men and women; but also masturbation, bestiality, rape, and child sexual abuse. Male friendship was generally felt to be more important than relationships between men and women. The love of men for men seems to have been accepted as a fact of life, and the language of male friendship in literature and the arts is passionate and often talks about same-sex love. In Shakespeare's plays, male bonding is sometimes shown to be bound up with aggression and with male erotic desire. And passionate female–female desire figures strongly in some of his comedies.

In religious and legal pronouncements, sodomy was treated as a heinous sin and a felony punishable by death, but it was rarely prosecuted. King James I was known for his male–male attachments – in a letter to one of his young lovers he writes: 'God bless you, my sweet child and wife [sic]. James'. Nicholas Udall was sacked as headmaster of Eton in the 1540s and prosecuted because 'he did commit buggery . . . sundry times'. However, this did not stop him being appointed headmaster at Westminster School some years later! The Lord Chancellor and essayist, Sir Francis Bacon, was quite open about his relationships with his male servants and was described in print, with little sense of disapproval, as a pederast.

Officially, homosexual activity was considered an abomination. There are numerous examples of statements of revulsion and hostility towards it in the abstract. But in practice, there seems to have been a tacit acceptance of male–male sex, particularly between men and their servants, and of male prostitution. Homosexuality certainly did exist on a considerable scale. Unless violence was involved or a same-sex act disrupted social order, the courts seem not have done much about it. One reason for this could be that since the average age for men to marry was in their late 20s and early 30s, homosexual behaviour was allowed as a form of birth control. With the population already rising at an alarming rate, there was an urgent need to stop young unmarried men from having sex with women – it needed to be kept in line with the economy's resources. Sex that didn't produce babies would have been one answer to the problem.

There was also a certain vagueness about lesbianism at the time. The law did not criminalise, or even recognize, lesbian acts. It was treated as something implausible but it was nevertheless practised, and awareness of female–female desire certainly existed. There were increasing references to it throughout the 16th and 17th centuries. A woman convicted of sodomy with a man or woman was given a death sentence, just as men were. But not all sodomy statutes specified female–female acts, and where they did, few were actually prosecuted. A law expert writing just after Shakespeare's time said that a woman could only commit buggery with an animal, and that the only time a case was cited was 'a great Lady who had committed Buggery with a Baboon, and conceived by it'!

In *The Golden Age*, a play by Shakespeare's fellow dramatist, Thomas Heywood, the young women attending on the goddess Diana are paired off as lovers: 'Madam, we are all coupled / And twinn'd in love, and hardly is there any / That will be won to change her bedfellow'. Queen Elizabeth I, who ordered all her PR exercises to portray her as The Virgin Queen, once joked that she should marry a Princess and play the husband's part in the relationship.

# DILDOS AND THE REDISCOVERY OF THE CLITORIS

eferences in all kinds of literature of the time to dildos and women with unusually large clitorises all testify to a male anxiety about women's sexuality. This is the era of the 'rediscovery of the clitoris.' And the reason it has ramifications for our understanding of attitudes to sex in Shakespeare's time is that it had long been thought that women's sexual organs were simply inferior versions of men's sexual organs – turned inside out, and positioned inside, and not outside, the body. So the vagina and ovaries were thought to be the mirror images of the penis and testicles. (This notion of male and female anatomies fitted to one another was challenged by no less an authority than Leonardo da Vinci.) The rediscovery of the clitoris in 1559 (it was known to Greek medical writers but then somehow got forgotten) showed that a woman's pleasure could be outside the control of a man. This is probably why there are so many references to dildos in the plays and pamphlets of the time.

There is a wonderfully funny poem by Thomas Nashe, 'The Choice of Valentines [Dildos]' in which the Beloved tells her lover he's lousy in bed and anyway, she doesn't need him anymore. 'Henceforth no more will I implore thine aid, / My little dildo shall supply their kind'. But the poem's comedy is shaded over by touches of male anxiety about the idea that men might be surplus to requirements (see page 236).

# FEMALE TRANSVESTITES

omen in masculine dress were quite a frequent sight and were the subject of puritanical outrage. The most famous female cross-dresser was Mary Frith, who was not only a petty crook, but a brothel madam who supplied young women with men. One woman she supplied with upper-class customers had twelve children and only the first of them was her husband's! Frith was, by her own account, the star of the London underworld, and in 1611 appeared at the Fortune Theatre wearing boots, breeches and sword, singing and playing the lute.

For us, the strange thing about these women who wore male clothing is that they weren't trying to be masculine. They dressed in men's attire because they saw it as empowering, as a bid for freedom from the rules laid down for them by men. It was a way of putting up two fingers to the establishment, and saying 'I have the sexual freedom to do what I like'. There is a remarkable description of such women dressed in male attire with their tops undone, flaunting their female attributes. They wore 'the loose, lascivious civil embracement of a French doublet being all but unbuttoned to entice [i.e. to reveal their breasts] ... most ruffianly short hair' and a sword. There were many moralists at the time who inveighed against the practice.

Shakespeare's reply to their outrage was to outrage them further by getting his women to dress up as men. Most striking of all would have been if they wore their jackets open with their breasts on show and wore a codpiece which would make them look as though they were walking around with a permanent erection. Shakespeare has a whole scene in *The Two Gentlemen of Verona* where the heroine Julia is discussing with her waiting-woman the making of her male costume so she can dress up in disguise (see pages 164–166). Much is made of the need to wear a codpiece, the padded pouch men wore to cover their genitals. This is a crucial part of Shakespeare's meaning. In his day, 'nothing' was a pun on female genitals meaning 'no thing', that is to say, no penis between a woman's legs. So the sight of a woman in male clothes, her breasts on show, and the highly suggestive addition of a 'penis' would have presented a striking image of a double-sexed being.

It was not illegal for women to dress in men's clothes, but there was a growing moral disapproval of female transvestites during the reign of James I, whose own wife favoured male attire.

# COCKNEYS AND CUCKOLDS

The theatre acquired a reputation for homosexuality during this time. In a play by Shakespeare's friend and fellow playwright, Ben Jonson, a father is horrified that his son is going to be an actor: 'What? Shall I have my son a stager now, an ingle [passive male homosexual] for players?' And one commentator wrote that 'a sodomite' is someone 'who is at every play and every night sups with his ingles'.

It's important to realise that the word 'effeminate' did not have the same connotations that it does today – in fact, it had a quite different significance. It meant men who were too much influenced by women, not a sign of homosexuality. Although it could be used to describe men who were not only emasculated by women but also had homoerotic tendencies. The very word suggests a process of 'feminising'. Shakespeare's Sonnets to the so-called 'Dark Lady' picture the woman's vagina as 'hell', and lust for her as something nauseating because it effeminates the lover. In the Middle Ages and the Renaissance men thought women were more lecherous than they were. This helps to explain the absolute obsession at the time with the notion of men being cuckolded by their wives. References to the subject are found more than once in at least sixteen of Shakespeare's plays, and everywhere in the works of other playwrights. It was thought a man's wild passion for a woman was dangerous, that it diminished his manhood. A Cockney was a Mummy's boy who became an effeminate male.

There are also many representations of erotic desire between women in the plays and literature of the time. The relationships between the pairs of female friends in *A Midsummer Night's Dream* and *As You Like It* are charged with erotic tension and longing. From the 1800s right up until the 1950s, directors of *A Midsummer Night's Dream* would routinely cut the most erotic lines of Helena's impassioned speech about her childhood friend, Hermia (see page 174). In *Twelfth Night* the heroine, Viola, dresses up as a boy and becomes the object of sexual desire for Countess Olivia. But instead of her cross-dressing making her look like a man, it is her feminine features that Olivia dwells lovingly on.

Shakespeare was fascinated with the ways in which disguise can act as a kind of catalyst for sexual desire – the irony of how a false identity can release your true identity.

## THE PLAY-BOYS: ALLURING TO MEN AND WOMEN

The boy-actor in his sexual disguise as a woman seems to have held an attraction for people of both sexes in the audience. Things get very complicated when female characters disguise themselves as boys, as Rosalind does in *As You Like It*. This whole question of 'Boys Will Be Girls Will be Boys' on Shakespeare's stage is a fascinating one. And he exploits the attendant sexual ambiguity to the hilt. When in *Twelfth Night*, Viola is dressed as the boy Cesario, attracting the amorous attentions of Olivia, the sexual punning Shakespeare employs imbues their exchanges with fairly broad hints of lesbianism. Similarly, Viola's disguise as a boy, a page to the Duke Orsino, creates another example of sexual ambiguity, by showing Orsino's attraction to the boy. Moments of tenderness between the man Orsino and the boy Cesario are charged with a homoerotic tension that is only really evident in a live performance. There are many such moments in Shakespeare, where homoerotic desire hovers over and between the characters, and takes the sexuality of the relationship to the edge.

Shakespeare was by no means alone in exploring the dramatic use of sexual disguise. Before London theatres were shut down by the Puritans in 1642, boy-actors disguised as girls disguised as boys appeared in at least 75 plays by almost 40 different playwrights, although many of these are believed to have copied ideas originated with Shakespeare. And they certainly did not treat the subject with the same subtlety.

The boy who originally played Shakespeare's Cleopatra must have been a superb actor. A great misconception about the abilities of the boy-actors is that female actors would have played the women's parts better, a view that has been unhelpfully reinforced by the film *Shakespeare in Love* (1998), in which the boy-actor cast to play Juliet is unable to act convincingly, and has to be replaced by a woman (played by Gwyneth Paltrow). But there is nothing to suggest that this was so. Indeed the opposite seems to have been the case. The English travel writer Thomas Coryate visited a playhouse in Venice where women played the female roles and wrote: 'I saw women act . . . and they performed it *with as good a grace*, action, gesture and whatsoever convenient for a player, as ever I saw any masculine actor' [author's italics].

Although Cleopatra doesn't take on a male disguise like Rosalind and Viola, Shakespeare makes her draw our attention to the fact she is being played by a boy. Before she dies, she predicts that 'Some squeaking Cleopatra [will] boy my greatness' (5.2). As Shakespeare's most alluring figure of female erotic power, Cleopatra dominates the play. She even has the final act all to herself because Antony dies in Act 4. To pull such a part off, the boy actor playing her must have been utterly compelling.

# WOMEN WIN THE PRIZE
# FOR RAUNCHY PUNNING

It is worth mentioning that though there may not have been women on the stage, there were plenty of them in the audience – visitors from abroad were shocked at how many there were. A Swiss tourist was amazed at the freedom women enjoyed in Elizabethan London. They went everywhere, he said – to Paris Garden, to the plays, and to the taverns and ale-houses, sometimes without a male escort. They had 'the key of the street', and did not have to veil their charms or forego their pleasures.

Shakespeare's heroines are all expert practitioners of the sexual pun, and in their 'wit contests' with male characters are always shown to be cleverer, more mature, and wittier – they invariably win the contest. There is plenty of evidence that in Shakespeare's day men and women spoke freely about sex with one another, and that women actively instigated talk about it.

Plays by Shakespeare's fellow writers all have female characters talking about fucking, pricks, cunts, ejaculation and buggery. There was certainly no concession, then, to any notion of a 'female sensibility' which might have taken offence at the vulgar puns of the plays.

# SHAKESPEARE'S APPEAL TO EVERY CLASS

In fact, the playgoers covered the whole social spectrum. The labourers and apprentices paid a penny to stand in the yard (Hamlet calls them 'penny stinkards'); the more affluent got seats on the three levels for two pennies; the more privileged middle classes paid six pennies to sit in private boxes nearest the stage called the 'gentlemen's rooms' – often filled with country gentlemen and their wives down or up to London on business from the provinces, and taking in a show). Finally, there were the aristocrats who paid a shilling to sit in the Lords' Room above the stage. Shakespeare's plays, then, were written for the widest possible audience. Given that as well as writing great drama, he also wanted to make money and wouldn't have risked offending any section of it, it seems that all his playgoers appreciated racy double entendres and coarse jokes.

# PROFOUND PUNS

Perhaps we've ignored this side of Shakespeare because he has become our major literary icon, a genius to be revered and placed on a pedestal, and, worshipping at the shrine, we like to keep him pure and unsullied.

But this is to do him a great disservice. His towering greatness resides in his matchless understanding of the human condition, his profound insights into the operations not only of the broad sweep of psychology, philosophy and politics, but also of greed, fear, jealousy, hatred, self-loathing, self-estrangement, friendship, sex, and, of course, love, in all its many hues. And when he came to explore all the facets of what it is to be human, he often chose to do so by means of sexual wordplay.

The most extreme examples of the plays' tantalising coded subtext range from uproarious *Carry On* double entendres to dazzling wordplay celebrating the exuberance of life, to profoundly moving expressions of a soul in pain.

# THE SECRET WORLD OF SPIES AND COUNTER-SPIES AND DOUBLE AGENTS

Shakespeare loved cloaking meanings for his audiences to decode. The English of the time were obsessed with deciphering codes. This is the period in English political history when, in response to growing plots to assassinate Elizabeth I, a national and international 'secret service' was born – what we now call MI5 and MI6. The secret world of spies and counter-spies, double agents and all those dirty games of infiltration and betrayal was being layered, if you like, into the fabric of Elizabethan society. Coded messages, concealment and disguise were used not just for political means, but for trade dealings about the price and importing of goods, for example. Invisible ink, made from urine, onion-juice, milk and orange-juice, was a favourite method of secret communication. Shakespeare tapped into this fascination, frequently offering lines that he knew would cause a delicious tingling down the spines of his playgoers.

# UNLOCKING THE KEY TO SECRET CODES

There is no doubt that much of Shakespeare's sexual wordplay is seductive – the irresistible allure of coded meanings, secret intimacies, shades of suspicion, insinuated significances, concealed emotions, suggestive hints. His acute awareness of how to draw an audience into the innermost feelings of his characters by making the playgoers' imagination take part in the whole dramatic experience, is something he brings to his use of puns.

And perhaps the truly startling aspect, for us, of his sexual punning vocabulary is how many words could be used for one underlying meaning. In addition to his relatively well-known synonyms for and about female genitals such as ring, rose, and thing, there are more than 180 others. A good many of these terms were also applied to the male genitals. As well as our familiar cock, prick, and balls, there are more than 200 words for male genitals. There are also more than 700 punning words and phrases on sex. The Appendix gives a list of these (see pages 296–300).

# THE CENSORS GET TO WORK

**B**ut in the years since his day, Shakespeare's most indecent sexual puns have been all but invisible in editions and performances of his plays, which has meant that the world has been deprived of a significant, and paradoxically serious, aspect of his work. We are also at a disadvantage, of course, because so many of the words of the time are not in our current vocabulary. Even ardent Shakespeare fans experience bum-numbing moments during long and apparently tedious exchanges of verbal banter that make little sense to us because we don't realize that the harmless-sounding words are actually exuberant displays of sparkling coded sexy dialogue.

Uneasiness about Shakespeare's sexual language really began in earnest just a few years after his death and led to censoring of the plays in the centuries that followed. Among his filthiest lines are Mercutio's insult about Rosaline: 'O Romeo, that she were, O that she were/An open-arse, and thou a popp'rin' pear' ('O' – vagina; 'popp'rin'' – pop her in). One edition, printed in his lifetime, replaced 'open-arse' with 'open *Et Caetera*', and a later one left a blank: 'open, or –', so censorship of Shakespeare's indecent language began when he was still writing his plays. Eighteenth-century editors cut the line out altogether. One editor thought it 'impossible' to read the love Sonnets addressed to a Young Man 'without an equal mixture of disgust and indignation', and another changed all the pronouns in these poems from he to she, so that the Poet's expressions of love were all safely addressed to a woman.

In the 19th century, Henrietta Bowdler and her brother Thomas cut out every obscenity in the works from her Family Shakespeare (giving rise to the term 'bowdlerise' for removing phrases or words regarded as indecent). Even the poet W.H. Auden, himself a homosexual, dodged the issue of the erotic nature of the Shakespeare Sonnets addressed to a Young Man, telling his friends in the early 1960s that 'it won't do just yet to admit that the Top Bard was in the homintern'. Even an edition of the Sonnets published in 1986 describes the poems to the youth as growing 'out of comradely affection in the literature of friendship'. Today, school editions of Shakespeare have great chunks of the plays missing. Whether schoolchildren would enjoy their Shakespeare lessons more if they were allowed to giggle and snigger at his sexual puns is a moot point.

When today's productions of the plays bring out the bawdy undertones, it has, with some exceptions, tended to be restricted to the less salacious puns (usually with a catch-all gesture indicating a penis or a grabbing at a woman's crotch) and safely confining them to 'low-life' comic characters.

But it's important to realise that Shakespeare did not confine his sexual puns to his clowns and fools. Kings, queens, princes, princesses and aristocrats are all expert dealers in the raciest double entendres. And the puns are found in every genre Shakespeare used – histories, tragedies, comedies, dark 'problem' comedies, and romances.

# SHAKESPEARE'S SEXUAL PUNS SIZZLE

hakespeare's sexual puns are sometimes simple, often complex, and range from the cheeky and playful to the blatantly filthy. But even the most light-hearted are rarely pointless. A ribald joke on cunt, arse, buggery or fucking (often all four) is invariably a means of revealing character, creating mood and tone, exploring the moral world of a play, or even forwarding the action.

He can offer straightforward, obvious sexual quibbles like other playwrights of the time, but he often does something more. He could make puns finely-tuned instruments for expressing subtle, ambiguous interpretations of a character or a situation where we are not quite sure of the precise meaning – just like life, in fact. Creative, inventive, clever wit makes many of his sexual puns sizzle.

But perhaps more than anything else, Shakespeare uses puns because, quite simply, they are more entertaining than using the real word. When his larger-than-life comic character, Sir John Falstaff, reminisces about visiting brothels in his youth, he tells how his friend 'came ever in the rearward fashion', the very politeness and tasteful etiquette of the phrase is completely at odds with what it's describing. If Shakespeare had written, 'came ever in the sodomite's fashion' not only would it not be all that funny, but it would deprive the audience of 'translating' the word 'rearward' for themselves.

Whenever the mischievous, 'merry' (horny) Puck, the fairy in *A Midsummer Night's Dream*, opens his mouth, you can be sure out will stream a superabundance of sexy puns, many of them sailing very close to the wind. And he likes nothing better than describing in every detail his sexual exploits. In one speech he tells us that, 'Sometime lurk I in a gossip's bowl ... against her lips I bob / And on her wither'd dewlap pour the ale ...' ('dewlap' – vaginal lips).

Shakespeare always requires his audience to do some work, whether it's pondering the legitimacy of a 'just war', as in *Henry V*, considering whether monarchs have a divine right to rule, as in *Richard II*, or questioning whether a young man has the right to ask his sister to give up her chastity to save his life, as in *Measure for Measure*. In all these serious matters, Shakespeare uses sexual wordplay to help his overall dramatic purpose in exploring human behaviour and inviting his audience to explore it with him. Shakespeare knew, more than any other dramatist, that the way to get your audience to think was to entertain them first.

# THE BARD MAKES UP A NEW WORD OR TWO, OR THREE THOUSAND AND COUNTING

Playing on words was one way of expressing the sheer variety of forms a language could use for describing actions and emotions. Shakespeare, more than all his fellow writers, was fascinated with words and what they could do. He became so frustrated at what he saw as the limited number of words available to him that he invented something like 3,000 new ones, and probably more. You can see how he progressively expanded his vocabulary to meet his demands for pinpointing a particular emotion, to hit just the right spot to show a character's take on life, to convey a nuance of meaning. It's been estimated that he had a vocabulary of 29,000 words – today, a British university graduate has between 3,000 and 4,000.

One intriguing question is that if Shakespeare invented so many new words, how did his audiences understand their meanings? He was too good a playwright to have risked pitching his plays above the playgoers' heads with a vocabulary they could not understand (and would not have been keen to reduce his company's takings). It seems that, in keeping with every aspect of his relationship with his audiences, Shakespeare never underestimated their intelligence. He must have been confident that their natural ability to understand the workings of rhetoric and their enthusiastic eagerness to embrace new words would enable them to get his meaning. And besides, Shakespeare would often provide a new word's meaning either by context or by subtly inserting it within its surrounding line or lines. He did the same whenever he employed a classical allusion that many in his audience may not have recognised. In *The Tempest*, you don't need to know Ceres is the goddess of earth and agriculture because she is described as the bounteous lady of the fruits of the earth. Shakespeare always had too much respect for his audience to believe that they could not meet whatever challenge he presented them with.

# SEXUAL PUNS GET SERIOUS

oday, our conception of language itself is very different. Like most people of the time, Shakespeare felt the power and force of words on his pulses: they were not just representations of things – they were experienced as the thing itself. Words were concrete, physical. In his dark comedy *Measure for Measure*, evil for Angelo, the corrupt deputy ruler, is not some abstract force 'out there'. His self-loathing caused by his sexual urge for a young novice nun becomes concrete, something powerfully physical – it is, he says, 'a strong and swelling evil'. The sexual pun here is, of course, on the literal meaning of what lust does – the swelling of his penis, and it's a powerful example of the way Shakespeare often uses sexual puns to explore complex moral questions.

When Hamlet, grieving for his dead father, revulsed by his mother's marriage to his uncle, cannot get repugnant images of sex out of his head, he uses dirty puns. We, the audience, listen as his obscene thoughts about his mother, Gertrude, become ever more indecent until we are imagining her being saturated in the filth of her son's mind. We are made to sense his feelings right to his final image of her having sex with her new husband like a copulating pig in a sty.

By no means all of Shakespeare's bawdy wordplay is on sex itself. He employs it to explore the bigger questions of philosophy, politics and morality. When Brutus in *Julius Caesar* urges his fellow conspirators to assassinate Caesar he uses sexual puns to express his moral passion. He says they do not need to swear an oath: 'What need we any spur [penis] but our own cause / To prick us to redress?' and he goes on to say he wants no weaklings, or venereally diseased oats [testicles] to stain their enterprise'. Shakespeare often uses clusters of puns and a developing pun to put across serious points. And many examples of his sexual subtext are subtle and romantic, delicate and poetic. Romeo describes Juliet's state of being ready for sexual awakening with puns on bud/maidenhead and ripe/sexually ready: 'This bud of love, by summer's ripening breath'.

# WHAT MAKES A PUN A
# SEXUAL ONE?

The most important point about any discussion of Shakespeare's sexual puns is that, apart from the obviously direct double meanings, when it comes to deciding whether a word has a ribald sexual subtext, context is everything. Who says it? Who is it being said to? Why? What is the tone of the passage?

There's a whole range of possible inflections of obscenity in the sexual puns of Shakespeare, from obvious broad comedy to rancid terms of abuse, to subtle shadings of love, poignancy and tragedy.

My interpretation of these possible inflections has been based on my knowledge and understanding of the playwright's works, but perhaps more significantly, on my own experience as a dramatist.

My criteria for what does and does not constitute sexual wordplay starts and ends with context and tonal register. Hamlet's infamous command to Ophelia, to 'get thee to a nunnery', is almost certainly intended to signal the word's double meaning of convent and brothel – nunnery as meaning 'brothel' is dated 1503 in the *Oxford English Dictionary*. Hamlet's words in the entire scene play on the theme of prostitution and sexually active women: 'bawd', 'breeder of sinners', 'I'll give thee this plague [VD] for thy dowry'... 'To a nunnery, go – and quickly [quick-fuck, get sexually aroused]'. Shakespeare changed English drama forever when he created Hamlet and showed how a character's language can often be saying several things at once, and contradictory meanings at that, to reflect fragmented thoughts and disturbed feelings.

This is a typical example of Shakespeare's technique of making the audience experience two meanings at once to powerful effect. If Hamlet simply says, 'Get thee to a brothel', we would lose the poignancy of the whole scene, and fail to register the warring emotions going on inside Hamlet's heart. The part of him who now thinks all women are whores because of his mother's 'incest' with his uncle, is treating Ophelia as a whore, but the side of him who loved, and possibly still loves her, is wanting her to go to a convent to preserve her chastity and be safe from marriage and the breeding of sinners. Shakespeare often reveals a character's divided self in this way, and achieves a psychological realism way ahead of its time. A further reason for taking 'nunnery' to have a double meaning is that, later in the play, Hamlet's words to Ophelia grow more and more coarse. He talks repeatedly of her cunt – 'country matters'; laying between 'maids' legs'; and later still, when Ophelia has gone mad, she sings obscene snatches of words echoing Hamlet's puns on nunnery.

## HOW OBSCENE IS THE PUN?

There may have been times, in Shakespeare's theatre, when the audience would decode a meaning that was not intended. There are certainly plenty of examples of characters making ribald puns without realising they are – and these can be the funniest moments of all. Mistress Quickly's unwitting double entendres make for some of the most laugh-out-loud scenes in Shakespeare.

It goes without saying that the words would also have been used quite harmlessly without a double meaning – talking about the beautiful colour of a rose when standing in a garden looking at one, is not likely to mean a character is using a double entendre for female genitals or a prostitute. Not everything that has a phallus shape denotes a prick, and not everything that is circular is a vagina or arsehole.

The word 'nothing' was a frequent pun on female genitalia, but this is not to say that every time Shakespeare used the word it had this significance. His audiences would have been able to distinguish between its bawdy and non-bawdy use. When, in the opening scene of *King Lear*, the King states his intention to divide up his kingdom between his three daughters, he asks them to enter what is basically a rhetoric contest – who can tell him they love him most. His youngest and favourite daughter, Cordelia, refuses to utter the false, empty rhetoric of her sisters. When he asks what she can say to top the praise of her sisters, she says one word: 'Nothing.' Clearly, Cordelia isn't pointing to her vagina when she says this word. Here, 'nothing' means only 'nothing'. There are plenty of words that, used in one context, have an underlining sexual significance, but none in another context.

As well as the question of being careful not to read a sexual pun where there probably isn't one, there is also the question of degree. With puns on female genitals that contain 'con' and 'coun', and elements that sound like cunt, such as 'quaint', one can assume that the underlying word is certainly 'cunt'. In Shakespeare's time, the word 'cunt' seems to have been a fairly common name for the vagina.

But what of other words like 'wit', 'lip', 'glove', 'cheveril' and the frequent 'ring' and 'O'? When does 'wit' suggest 'vagina', and when does it suggest 'cunt'? Again, context and tone are all. If it's the foul-mouthed Iago in *Othello* saying 'wit', it's reasonable to surmise that he's using it as a pun on 'cunt' and not the more polite 'vagina'. A character who is first introduced to us portrayed as having a pornographic mind, whose language is steeped in lurid descriptions of the heroine's sexual parts and obsessed with bestial images of her having sex – being 'tupped' by a 'black ram'; 'covered with a Barbary horse'; 'making the beast with two backs', is not going to deal in genteel punning.

Any discussion of the use of sexual puns in Shakespeare's day has to take into account that his audiences were far more sophisticated in their listening skills than we are, and that sexual punning was much more a part of normal discourse in everyday life. A playgoer would have been able to spot immediately whether a character's pun denoted a 'light' meaning or a racier one, or indeed, if it was not a pun at all. If, like many playgoers, you went to the theatre three or four times a week, you would have been expert at assessing the degree of obscenity intended by a sexual pun. The tone of the scene and characters involved would be your guide.

But the examples of sexual wordplay in this book obviously work in the same way as we use puns today – if we talk about a screw to describe only an object we're driving into the wall, it's clearly not a pun on fuck. In the same way, when an actor in Shakespeare shouts 'Away!', which often meant the equivalent of our 'Go fuck yourself!', or 'Whoreson' which is our 'Son-of-a-bitch', it isn't necessarily meant literally – we're not expecting the person to go and literally fuck themselves.

Shakespeare often uses language about sport and dancing to disguise (or reveal!) talk about sex. The effect is usually many layered. First, the harmless surface word, secondly, the sexual subtext beneath the spoken word, and this, in turn, revealing a third level – the cut-and-thrust dialogue which mimics the sex-act.

He loves the idea of representing the progression of sexual foreplay to climax by verbal repartee, so that the language makes the meaning. One character takes the word of the other and finds a meaning in it that was not intended and flings it back with another meaning, in a bantering pattern that gets more and more sexy. Every single conversation between Petruchio and Katherine in *The Taming of the Shrew* is a finely orchestrated example of this.

It is an obvious point, but the fact that the words are uttered by actors who can convey the sexual hints and significances of the puns with all manner of vocal nuances, accompanied by movement, gestures, expression, even touch, allows the bawdy meanings to come alive for the audience in a way that is clearly not possible when the words are trapped on the printed page. An obvious example is when an actor uses a pause so that the audience fills in the line with a sexually charged pun before the actor completes the line with a harmless, or less bawdy word: For example, here, when Quickly says 'There's neither faith, nor truth, nor womanhood in me . . .' the unspoken stage direction is a pause before '. . . else', so that it appears that she's saying there is no faith or truth or womanhood in her.

A major purpose of this book is to reinstate these long-lost meanings, and provide the key to opening up a whole new way of looking at Shakespeare. The more that the sexual undertones of Shakespeare's plays can be recovered the richer our experience of his works will be.

By ignoring many of these sexual puns we have been deprived of some of the funniest and, paradoxically, some of the most profoundly serious moments in Shakespeare. In the hands of the supreme dramatist sexual wordplay became a fine-tuned instrument with which to explore the full spectrum of human behaviour. It's time to unlock the meaning beneath the coded words.

What follows is a personal selection of extracts from the plays and poems given under different headings. The overall aim is not just to offer a modern 'translation' of the wordplay. This very often necessarily results in clumsy sentence structure and nearly always entails a loss of some element of the original such as the rhythm of the verse. In many cases, there are different words meaning the same thing to intensify the effect of the puns. The intention is for the reader to bring new knowledge of what the words mean and then return to Shakespeare's lines, when a full appreciation of how the sexual subtext is cleverly constructed and beautifully modulated will now be possible. The glossaries at the end of each entry provide the meanings so the readers can bring their own interpretations to the quotations.

Short introductions to each entry set down the context and characters, and many entries also offer some fascinating facts and details relating to a great variety of aspects of Shakespeare and his world. So, for example, in the chapter on 'Buggery', where Falstaff says that his friend Shallow 'came ever in the rearward fashion', I have traced in the legal situation regarding sodomy in Shakespeare's time, while in one of the entries pertaining to 'Cunt', the commentary shows how the playwright uses obscene puns to mimic the elaborate, choreographed foreplay and sexual intercourse between two characters who are ostensibly hurling insults at each other.

The subject of sex, same-sex sex, love, passion, pricks, cunts, wanking, ejaculation, impotence, finger-fucking, venereal disease, erections and dildos… all seem to have exerted a powerful fascination on Shakespeare's audiences. And they're all there – in tantalising code – in his plays.

# A NOTE ON SOURCES

Shakespeare is quoted from *The Norton Shakespeare: Based on the Oxford Edition* (1997); general editor, Stephen Greenblatt. I have used other editions for *Pericles, Henry VI Part One* and Sonnet 20. The quotations from the plays have been in many cases heavily edited, and in order to avoid unwieldy text break signs, ellipses have been kept to a minimum. The translations do not indicate breaks in the text.

In addition to the rich source of wordplay in the writings of Shakespeare's contemporaries, four reference books contain a wealth of information about language use in 16th- and 17th-century England. The compendious volume by lexicographer Randle Cotgrave, who meticulously recorded French and English in *A Dictionarie of the French and English Tongues* (1611); B.E.'s *A New Dictionary of the Terms Ancient and Modern of the Canting Crew in its Several Tribes of Gypsies, Beggars, Thieves, Cheats etc . . .* (1699); John Florio's *A Worlde of Words, or Most copious, and exact Dictionarie in Italian and Englishe* (1598), later expanded as *Queen Anna's New World of Words, or Dictionarie of the Italian and English Tongues* (1611); and the later collection of slang words, Francis Grose's *Dictionarie of the Vulgar Tongue* (1785). Other early modern dictionaries include John Palsgrave, English–French (1530); Sir Thomas Elyot, Latin–English (1538), and the first full English-only dictionary by Thomas Blount (1656).

These dictionaries are a gold-mine of details for sexual puns. It's important to bear in mind that very often words were only officially recorded in the *Oxford English Dictionary* long after they had already been in use for some time. The first record of the word 'cock' meaning 'penis', for example, is dated 1730 in the *OED*, when in fact, it had been in use for more like two hundred years. Also, the *OED* for early modern English words is far from complete and accurate because it overlooked the bilingual dictionaries like Cotgrave's monumental work and the other dictionaries listed above.

*Pertaining to*

# FUCKING

# EROTIC FOREPLAY
## LOVE'S LABOUR'S LOST
### Act 2, Scene 1

Shakespeare never actually used 'fuck' as a written word in his plays and poems, but he gave his audiences a bewildering number of puns on it, preferring to give them the tingle factor of decoding the double meanings.

Biron, the hero of *Love's Labour's Lost*, has been forced by the King of Navarre to join his friends in a vow to have nothing to do with women for three years and to devote themselves to study: 'No woman shall come [reach orgasm] within a mile of my court on pain of losing her tongue [clitoris].' But the Princess of France and her entourage, including the heroine, Rosaline, arrive to discuss urgent matters of state with the King, so the men have to give up their vow. Womaniser Biron, who'd doubted he could keep such a vow, is highly relieved.

*Love's Labour's Lost* is set in the royal court, a place where courtiers were expected to conduct themselves in a sedate and seemly manner, speak in polite, high-flown rhetoric and compose elegant love sonnets. Shakespeare, however, overturns courtly convention by cramming the play with an astonishing number of crude jokes and coarse sexual puns. Since these are generally uttered in poetic, flowery language, their real meaning is completely at variance with the manner in which it is expressed. Underlying obscenity punctuates the surface decorum.

Productions of the play that do not bring out the full meaning of its wordplay lead audiences to think they're just watching a group of poncey youths chasing a bunch of uppity girls, and Shakespeare's satire on the shallow values of the court is lost.

Every meeting between the men and women in *Love's Labour's Lost* is a wit contest, with sex as its subtext. This first contest between Biron and

Rosaline has a powerful sexual charge: tongues are like sharp swords that thrust and parry in rhythmic imitation of the sex act. When Rosaline skilfully deflects Biron's probes and 'wins' the fight, he gives up, attempting to cover up his humiliating 'defeat' by changing the subject and asking what the time is – only to become the butt of yet another caustic jibe. As always with Shakespeare, the woman proves to be cleverer, wittier and more vulgar than the man. And Shakespeare is at pains to show that Rosaline refuses to be cast in the role of passive partner. When Biron asks 'Didn't I fuck you?', Rosaline's word-for-word riposte is not mere repetition – she's insisting that *she* fucked him.

*Biron* Did not I dance with you in Brabant once?

*Rosaline* Did not I dance with you in Brabant once?

*Biron* I know you did.

*Rosaline*                How needless was it then
To ask the question!

*Biron*                You must not be so quick.

*Rosaline* 'Tis 'long of you, that spur me with such questions.

*Biron* Your wit's too hot, it speeds too fast, 'twill tire.

*Rosaline* Not till it leave the rider in the mire.

*Biron* What time o' day?

*Rosaline* The hour that fools should ask.

*Biron* Didn't I fuck you in the genitals once?

*Rosaline* Didn't I fuck *you* in the genitals once?

*Biron* I know you fucked me.

*Rosaline* How pointless was it to ask the question then!

*Biron* You mustn't be so quick to get aroused.

*Rosaline* It's because you insist on pricking me with your probings.

*Biron* Your cunt's too hot, it climaxes too fast, it'll tire.

*Rosaline* Not till it leave the one who's mounted me in the shit.

*Biron* What's the time?

*Rosaline* The time when pricks ask you what the time is.

Dance. To fuck. {'Dancing school' was a name for a brothel}

Brabant. The Low Countries, the Netherlands. {Used as a pun for the 'nether regions', i.e. the genitals}

Quick. Sexually aroused.

Spur. To prick, to fuck.

Questions. Sexual probings.

Wit. Cunt.

Speeds. Climaxes.

Fast. To fuck.

Rider. Someone who 'mounts' their sexual partner.

Mire. Shit.

Fool. Prick.

The word 'Dance' in the sense of 'fuck' also crops up in the phrase 'Dance with one's heels', used by Shakespeare in *Much Ado About Nothing*, 3.4. The phrase refers to a woman thumping her heels against the bed during sex in time with the thrusts of her partner. In *Henry V*, 3.5, when the Dauphin complains: 'Our madams [whores] mock at us, and plainly say our mettle [semen] is bred out [knackered]', the Duke of Bourbon adds: 'They bid us "To the English dancing-schools [brothels]" ... Saying our grace [penis] is only in our heels.'

The word 'wit' is spoken more often in *Love's Labour's Lost* than in any other Shakespearean work, and almost always carries with it the punning meaning of 'cunt', 'vagina' or 'genitals'. This sexual connotation has multiple sources, including the word 'white' in the sense of a target in archery, and the phrase 'no whit' meaning 'not at all', in which the word 'all' was pronounced as 'hole'.

This plethora of punning and wordplay reflects a central theme of the play – that sexual language is used as a substitute for sexual action. It's like displacement therapy: the characters are always talking about sex but never do anything about it. The whole dramatic drive of the play is an exquisitely choreographed act of erotic foreplay with the actual sex act deferred.

# A QUICK KNEE-
# TREMBLER

## THE WINTER'S TALE

### *Act 3, Scene 3*

A man sees his wife talking to his best friend and suddenly explodes with irrational jealousy. He accuses her of being pregnant by him.

In one of the most terrifying paroxysms of jealous rage in all of Shakespeare, Leontes utters a stream of obscenities. He has his heavily pregnant wife put on trial and imprisoned, and when the baby is born orders it to be murdered saying: 'The bastard's brains with these my proper hands/ Shall I dash out ... Shall I live on, to see this bastard ... call me father? Better burn it now.' He orders the baby girl to be taken to a remote, inhospitable place, where she will almost certainly be killed by wolves and bears. Here, the baby is found by an old shepherd:

*Old Shepherd* What have we here? Mercy on's, a bairn!

A very pretty bairn. A boy or a child, I wonder? A

pretty one, a very pretty one. Sure some scape. Though

I am not bookish, yet I can read 'waiting-gentlewoman'

in the scape. This has been some stair-work, some

trunk-work, some behind-door-work. They were

warmer that got this than the poor thing is here.

*Old Shepherd* What have we here? Mercy on us, a baby! A boy or a girl, I wonder? It's a very pretty one. It's certain to be the result of some naughty fucking. I might not be able to read books, but I can read the meaning of this. I can see that this is a classic case of a serving-woman in trouble. We're talking about a shag behind the back stairs, a furtive fuck inside a trunk or a quick screw up against a wall. And while they were at it, the couple who conceived this child were a lot warmer than this poor thing is now.

Scape. Naughty fucking. {The phrase 'Waiting-gentlewoman in the scape' alludes to the many stories in popular songs and pamphlets of the time of servant-women abandoning or even killing their illegitimate children}
Stair work. Clandestine fucking behind the stairs. {The suggestion is of a 'knee-trembler', i.e. sex in a standing position}
Trunk work. Clandestine fucking inside a trunk.
Behind-door-work. A quick screw up against a wall. {Again, the suggestion is of a 'knee-trembler', sex in a standing position}
Got. Conceived.

Shakespeare's first child, conceived out of wedlock, was the result of some kind of 'stair work'. His hasty marriage to Anne Hathaway certainly suggests so. Although an unmarried mother would not have been stigmatised to the extent she would have been in Victorian times, there was still social disapproval and a certain amount of shame surrounding bastardy in Shakespeare's day.

There are several reluctant bridegrooms in Shakespeare who are forced to marry the women they've made pregnant. Armado in *Love's Labour's Lost*, 5.2, is told by the clown Costard that his peasant girlfriend 'is two months on her way' and unless he marries her, the poor wench will become a social outcast. 'The child brags in her belly. 'Tis yours', says Costard.

*Henry VI, Part One*, 5.7, contains another reference to forced marriages: 'For what is wedlock forced but a hell,/ An age of discord and continual strife.'

# THE VAGINA DIALOGUES

## THE MERRY WIVES OF WINDSOR

### Act 4, Scene 1

The only time we actually hear the word 'fuck' in Shakespeare is here, in a wonderfully obscene mock-lesson in Latin grammar in which the Welsh accent of a schoolmaster pronounces the letter 'v' in the word 'vocative' as an 'f', and the word is *sounded* loud and clear.

Shakespeare creates a whole scene revolving around the sexual connotations of Latin word endings. These change in form depending on their 'case' – that is, their grammatical function within the sentence. The nominative case, for instance, expresses the subject of a statement ('*Shakespeare* is a playwright'), while the accusative case expresses the direct object of a verb ('Shakespeare wrote *plays*'). The vocative case, with which Shakespeare makes great play here, is used to address someone or something in direct speech ('*O Shakespeare!* Write a filthy play!').

The lewdness of the scene is increased by the repetition of the letter 'O' which, like any word to do with circles or holes, was one of the commonest punning terms for female genitals in Shakespeare's day. The lewd meaning of 'O' is reinforced by the frequent appearances of the word 'case', which also meant 'cunt'. Throughout the scene the schoolmaster is comically unaware of the sexual subtext of what he's saying. The schoolboy, meanwhile, is loving every minute of pronouncing the obscenities and Shakespeare's implied stage direction to the actor is that he's stifling naughty-schoolboy sniggers.

Here he is then, the schoolboy tellingly named William, turning a boring Latin grammar lesson into a gloriously indecent feast of sexual puns.

✝

*Evans* What is he, William, that does lend articles?

*William* Articles are borrowed of the pronoun, and be thus declined . . . '*hic, haec, hoc*'.

*Evans* What is the focative case, William?

*William* O - *vocativo*, O -

*Evans* Remember, William, focative is *caret* . . . What is your genitive case plural, William?

*William* Genitive case?

*Evans* Ay.

*William* *Genitivo*: '*horum, harum, horum*'.

✝

*Evans* What is he, William, that bends his genitals for fucking?

*William* Genitals are borrowed of the pronoun and are thus declined: 'he fucks, she fucks, it fucks'.

*Evans* What is the fucking vagina, William?

*William* Cunt - vocativ-Cunt, Cunt -

*Evans* Remember, William, focative is penis. What is your genitive case plural, William?

*William* The genitals' genital?

Genitiv-Cunt: 'of masculine whores, of feminine whores, of 'neuter' whores'.

Lend. To bend over for sex.

Articles. Genitals.

*Hic, haec, hoc.* The masculine, feminine and neuter forms of 'this' in Latin. {Punning on the English words 'hick' and 'hack', which in Shakespeare's time meant 'fuck', 'bonk' or 'shag'}

Caret. Carrot, i.e. a penis.

Case. Vagina, cunt.

Genitive. Genitals.

Horum. Whore.

The repetition of puns on genitals, together with William's increasing daring in his mockery of the schoolmaster, suggests that the audience would have imagined the subtext to become progressively more indecent – from genitals, to vagina, to cunt.

A fellow playwright, Ben Jonson, mocked Shakespeare's 'small Latin, less Greek', but it is as well to bear in mind that when Shakespeare left school his standard of Latin would have been the equivalent of a university honours graduate's today.

Shakespeare would have spent twelve hours a day at school, six days a week, twelve months of the year. Lessons started at 6 a.m. (7 a.m. in winter) and went on until 11 a.m., with a short pause for breakfast. Work began again at 1 p.m. and lasted until 6 p.m. Apart from instruction in the articles of the Christian faith, all lessons would have consisted of Latin study – a gruelling schedule of vocabulary and grammar, and analysis and imitation of Classical texts.

Through the schoolboy, William, Shakespeare is clearly exacting retribution for the interminable days spent inside the schoolroom of his childhood, where he must have shared such dirty jokes in surreptitious whispers with his schoolmates behind the master's back.

# COCK-SURE WILL

## Sonnet 135

As chat-up lines go, this must be amongst the most obscene. This is a send-up of the Love Sonnet where, traditionally, the Poet praises the coldly aloof Beloved's *chastity* with sweet, flowery verse, in tones of reverential respect. In great contrast, here the inept would-be lover dwells on the promiscuous Beloved's large and capacious vagina that's been visited so often, there's surely room for one prick more?

The word 'Will' occurs thirteen times in this sonnet as a multi-layered pun on male and female sex organs, on sexual desire, and on 'Will' as a Christian name. 'Will' was italicised and capitalised seven times in the original edition, which is kept here. Will's own prick and his mistress's vagina get wonderfully entangled, in what almost amounts to an enactment of the sex act itself.

Whoever hath her wish, thou hast thy *Will*,

And *Will* to boot, and *Will* in overplus.

More than enough am I that vex thee still,

To thy sweet will making addition thus.

With thou, whose will is large and spacious,

Not once vouchsafe to hide my will in thine?

Shall will in others seem right gracious,

And in my will no fair acceptance shine?

The sea, all water, yet receives rain still,
And in abundance addeth to his store;
So thou, being rich in *Will*, add to thy *Will*
One will of mine to make thy large *Will* more.
  Let no unkind no fair beseechers kill;
  Think all but one, and me in that one *Will*.

†

While other women can only wish for sex, your sexual desires are fulfilled by your *Will*, and you'd get *Will*'s prick into the bargain, in fact you'd get an excess of *Will*'s fucking.

I can fuck you better than all your lovers put together and I'll keep on tormenting you with my sexual advances: I can add another prick to your sweet cunt.

Will you not, with that vagina of yours which is large and spacious from so much use by other men, just this once let me hide my prick in your cunt?

Are you saying that other men seem well-hung to you but you don't find my prick acceptable? The sea is all water, but it still receives rain, and adds to it abundantly. It's the same with you. Even though you're already rich in the pricks of all your lovers, I'm asking you to add my prick to your vagina – to make it even larger. My cock's already got a hard-on just by looking at you and now it's got bigger. Stop saying 'No', unkind lady, stop killing my perfectly reasonable sexual advances. Think of all your lovers as being a single one, and treat me as the only one you want to fuck, the sole occupier of your cunt - your *Will*.

Whoever hath her wish. While other women wish for sex.

Will. Christian name.

Will. Prick.

More than enough. Bragging that he can fuck better than all other lovers put together.

Will. Cunt, vagina.

Gracious. Well endowed with all the graces (i.e. genitals), well-hung.

Will. Sexual desire.

Will. In the last line, 'Will' puns on all four meanings: Christian name, prick, cunt, sexual desire.

The delightfully bawdy punning phrase 'buttered bun', used in Shakespeare's time to describe a woman who has had sex with one man and is about to repeat the act with another, is still in slang use today.

In Sonnet 136, Will the Poet enacts a striptease with words. The Poet is still bragging away about his cock, only this time the emphasis is on both its size and its uniqueness. He also seems to have acquired more pricks! And he's making the comic repetition of the word 'Will' even more ridiculous. Will, the Poet, tells the lady: I will satisfy your sexual desire/ fill your vagina to the brim with pricks. Only I can do this.

*Pertaining to*

# CUNT

# A MOIST HOSPITABLE VAGINA

## THE TAMING OF THE SHREW

### Act 4, Scene 3

There are so many different words for female genitalia in Shakespeare - a good many of them particularly filthy - that we are spoilt for choice.

'Con-' and 'coun' at the beginning of any word was often a pun on 'cunt'. 'Con' is French for 'cunt' and the French pronunciation of the English 'gown' sounds like 'coun'. One of the funniest scenes playing on the word 'gown' is in *The Taming of the Shrew*, where the heroine defends the shape and beauty of her genitals against male mockery.

Katherine is the eldest daughter of a widower who treats her appallingly. He encourages his friends to insult her, calling her a witch, a devil, stark mad and evil because she has the effrontery to refuse to conform to their idea of the perfect woman – she speaks her mind and is determined never to marry. Her sister, Bianca, is the opposite, all submissive smiles, with many suitors. But Bianca cannot marry until Katherine does, and each of her suitors despairs of being able to wed her because it's quite obvious to them that no man in his right mind would marry Katherine.

Enter Petruchio, a larger-than-life gold-digger, 'come to wive it wealthily in Padua'. He hears about 'The Shrew' Katherine and her large dowry, and immediately decides he'll woo and win her. Katherine has met her match. Having married Katherine, Petruchio attempts to browbeat her into submission. Here he finds fault with her new 'gown'.

*Petruchio* Lay forth the gown . . .

O mercy, God, what masquing stuff is here?

What's this - a sleeve? 'Tis like a demi-cannon.

What, up and down carved like an apple-tart? . . .

Why, what i'devil's name, tailor, call'st thou this? . . .

*Katherine* I never saw a better fashioned gown,

More quaint, more pleasing, nor more commendable.

*Petruchio* Lay out the cunt. God Almighty! This is the
sort of over-the-top thing you'd wear to a fancy-dress
party! What's this - a sleeve? It's like a huge six-
incher. What, cut like a tart's cunt, good for sexual
thrusts? Why, what in the devil's name, tailor, do
you call this?

*Katherine* I never saw a cunt better fitted to provoke
male orgasms, a more well-endowed cunt, more capable
of giving sexual pleasure, or more praiseworthy.

Gown. Cunt.

Demi-cannon. A large gun, six inches long.

Up and down. A reference to sexual thrusts.

Carved. Cut, another pun on cunt.

Apple-tart. Tart.

Fashioned. Punning on 'fashion' as a word for penis. {From the Latin *fascinum*, penis}

Quaint. Cunt. {More than two centuries before, the word was used by Chaucer, best known for his bawdy *Canterbury Tales*: 'And prively he caughte hire by the queynte'}

Women's gowns and petticoats at the time had openings called plackets that gave access to the genital area. No underwear was worn at the time by women or men, so plackets, like codpieces, gave instant access, as it were. The word 'placket' thus acquired obvious sexual connotations and was used as a pun on the vagina.

In *King Lear*, 3.4, Edgar, the son of Lear's friend Gloucester, warns men to have nothing to do with women: 'Keep thy foot [punning on 'fuck'] out of brothels, thy hand out of plackets.'

When the Clown in *The Winter's Tale*, 4.3, bemoans the loose behaviour of young women, he says: 'Will they wear their plackets where they should bear their faces?'

# THE SULPHROUS PIT

## KING LEAR

### *Act 4, Scene 6*

It is one of the most shocking and harrowing invectives against the female vulva in all literature. King Lear, gone terrifyingly mad, screams obscenities against women.

The speech, with its pathological loathing of female sexuality, expresses Lear's pain at being rejected by two of his daughters, and his horror at what he sees as a world brutalised and corrupted.

Describing a woman's face (cunt), he says that neither a polecat (prostitute) nor a horse on heat fucks with a grosser sexual appetite.

✝

*King Lear* Down from the waist they are Centaurs,

Though women all above.

But to the girdle do the gods inherit.

Beneath is all the fiends'; there's hell, there's darkness,

There's the sulphurous pit, burning, scalding,

Stench, consumption! Fie, fie, fie . . . !

✝

*King Lear* Down from the waist they're monsters who have sex with beasts. But they're all women above. The gods own their bodies only down to their waists. Beneath their waists, everything belongs to the evil devils. There's hell, there's darkness, there is the sulphurous cunt, burning, scalding with sexual heat, stinking from having sex, consumed by their own hot lust. I shit on them, shit on them, shit on them!

Centaurs. Referring to bestiality: Lear imagines his daughters having sex with beasts. {Centaurs were lecherous creatures in mythology, having a human body above the waist and the legs and torso of a horse below it}

Girdle. Waist.

Fiend. Devil.

Hell. Cunt. {See below}

Pit. Cunt.

Fie! Shit!

'Hell' is a term frequently used in Shakespeare's time for female genitals. The playwright uses it again in Sonnet 144 when the Poet imagines his female lover fucking his friend – the so-called 'Dark Lady' and 'Fair Youth':

> *'Suspect I may, yet not directly tell . . .*
> *I guess one angel in another's hell.'*

'Put the devil into hell' was a phrase for sexual intercourse coined by the Italian author Boccaccio in the *Decameron* (1353).

# SPELLING IT OUT
## TWELFTH NIGHT,
### *Act 2, Scene 5*

One of Shakespeare's best jokes on prissy puritanical party-poopers is to have made a Puritan spell out the word 'cunt' on the public stage.

In *Twelfth Night* Shakespeare makes one of his frequent digs at the Puritans who were constantly attacking the theatre and trying to have the playhouses closed down.

The gloriously odious Malvolio is the steward of the rich Countess Olivia, whom he dreams of marrying. Shakespeare's satire on the Puritans even extends to Malvolio's name, which means 'ill will'. And his job title contains a further demeaning sexual pun, as 'steward' could also mean 'pimp'.

Olivia's debauched uncle, a drunken aristocrat fittingly named Sir Toby Belch (Fart), and her fool of a suitor, Sir Andrew Aguecheek (Pox-arse), overhear Malvolio talking to himself, fantasising that Olivia fancies him, and that he must be in with a chance with her. His absurdly narcissistic character makes him come out with a line that he doesn't realise is the ultimate insult to himself: 'O to be Count Malvolio!', which the audience hears as 'Cunt Malvolio!'.

Belch and Aguecheek decide to play a cruel trick on him. They forge a love letter to him as though written by Olivia, which commands him to appear before her in yellow (a colour she 'abhors') cross-gartered stockings (an old-fashioned way of adjusting a garter) and wearing a permanent smile. The scene, one of the funniest in all Shakespeare is always referred to as 'The Gulling of Malvolio'.

When he comes on stage dressed in the yellow stockings, with his face stiff with fixed smile, it always brings the house down.

*Malvolio* {*Taking up the letter*} By my life, this is my lady's hand. These be her very c's, her u's, and her t's, and thus makes she her great P's. It is in contempt of question her hand.

*Malvolio* {*Taking up the letter*} By my life, this is my lady's hand. These are her very C's, her U's, 'N' her T's, and thus makes she her great Piss. It is beyond question her masturbating hand.

C's, U's, and her T's. Cunt. {'Cut' is slang for cunt; the word 'and' was pronounced as an 'n'}

P's. Piss. Her hand. i.e. her masturbating hand.

Shakespeare has great fun in presenting Malvolio as one of the most loathsome, self-opinionated, arse-licking slime-balls of all his characters, with deeply unpleasant class envy and aspirations to social climbing thrown in. The Puritans waged an unceasing, virulent attack on the theatre and actors throughout the time of Shakespeare. In *The Anatomie of Abuses* (1583), the 'anti-theatrical' pamphleteer Philip Stubbes raged against what he saw as the theatre's sinful sexual provocation of playgoers:

'Do they not maintain bawdry . . . induce whoredowm and uncleanliness? Are they not plain devourers of maidenly virginity and chastity? For proof . . . mark the flocking and running to Theatres . . . to see plays and interludes, where such wanton gestures, such bawdy speeches, such laughing and . . . such kissing and bussing, such clipping and culling, such winking and glancing of wanton eyes, and the like, is used . . . Then these goodly [provocative] pageants being done, every mate sorts to his mate, every one brings another homeward . . . and in their secret conclaves (covertly) they play the Sodomites or worse . . .'

# PARLEZ-VOUS DE FILTH?

## HENRY V

### Act 3, Scene 4

A demure French princess discovers that a language lesson can send unexpected tingles down the spine.

The setting is an English lesson for the French Princess who will marry England's Henry V. Her chaperone, Alice, is teaching her the English words for parts of the body, but Catherine is completely unaware that her faulty pronunciations are producing double entendres. The punning grows progressively more obscene as the catalogue of sexual puns rises to its climax, accompanied by appropriate gestures as the Princess points to her body parts (so no one in the audience would have had to know French to get the puns). The opportunities for the actor playing Catherine to really work the crowd, make the scene a mini dramatic masterpiece.

The climax arrives when the Princess reaches the words 'foot' and 'gown'. *'Foutre'*, the French for 'fuck', was also used as a sexual pun by the English as 'foutra'. Catherine's pronunciation turns 'gown' into 'coun' to sound like 'cunt'. When she realises she has just said some 'very bad words', she first expresses horror, but clearly finds the experience deliciously thrilling: she immediately says them again ... at which point, she brings the house down.

*Catherine* Comment appelez-vous la main en anglais?

*Alice* . . . Elle est appelée de hand.

*Catherine* De hand. Et les doigts?

*Alice* . . . de fingres.

*Catherine* La main, de hand; les doigts, de fingres . . .
Comment appelez-vous les ongles?

*Alice* . . . de nails

*Catherine* De nails . . . le bras?

*Alice* De arma, madame.

*Catherine* Et le coude?

*Alice* D'elbow.

*Catherine* D'elbow . . . Écoutez: d'hand, de fingre,
de nails, d'arma, de bilbow . . . Comment appelez-vous
le col?

*Alice* De nick, madame.

*Catherine* De nick. Et le menton?

*Alice* De chin.

*Catherine* De sin. Le col, de nick; le menton, de sin . . .
D'elbow, de nick et de sin. Comment appelez-vous les
pieds et la robe?

*Alice* De foot, madame, et de cown.

*Catherine* De foot et de cown? O Seigneur Dieu! Ils sont
les mots de son mauvais, corruptible, gros, et
impudique, et non pour les dames d'honneur d'user.

Je ne voudrais prononcer ces mots devant les seigneurs
de France pour tout le monde. Foh! De foot et de cown!
Néanmoins, je réciterai une autre fois ma leçon
ensemble. D'hand, de fingre, de nails, d'arma, d'elbow,
de nick, de sin, de foot, de cown.

*Alice* Excellent, madame!

*Catherine* What do you call the hand in (obscene)
English?

*Alice* It is called the cock.

*Catherine* The cock. And the fingers?

*Alice* The pricks.

*Catherine* The hand, the cock; the fingers, the pricks.
What do you call the nails?

*Alice* The screws.

*Catherine* The screws. The arms?

*Alice* The cocks, my lady.

*Catherine* And the elbow?

*Alice* The knob.

*Catherine* The knob. Listen: The cock, the pricks,
the screws, the cocks and the knob. What do you call
the neck?

*Alice* The vagina, my lady.

*Catherine* The vagina. And the chin?

*Alice* The penis.

*Catherine* The penis. The neck, the vagina; the chin, the penis. The knob, the vagina and the penis. What do you call the robe and the gown?

*Alice* The fuck, my lady, and the cunt.

*Catherine* The fuck and the cunt? O Lord God! Those are very bad words. People could easily misconstrue them, they are vulgar and naughty, and not for respectable ladies to use. I wouldn't speak those words in front of French gentlemen for all the world. Still, I think I will recite my entire lesson one more time. The cock, the pricks, the screws, the cocks, the knob, the vagina, the penis, fuck and cunt.

*Alice* Excellently obscene, madam!

Hand. Prick. {Hand as a phallic symbol, and also suggesting 'holding' as in holding the 'hand' in masturbation}

Fingers. Pricks.

Nails. Screws.

Arms. Cocks.

Elbow. Catherine confuses 'elbow' with 'bilbow', an old word for a sword which puns on 'knob' or 'prick'.

Nick/Neck. Vagina. {In *Hamlet* 3.4, the hero – repulsed by his mother's remarriage – taunts her with the image of his stepfather 'paddling in your neck with his damned fingers'}

Chin. Penis. {The protruding part

of the jaw. A dictionary of the time refers to the Latin name for chin, *mentum* for '*mentule*' - man's yard or penis}

Foot. This would sound like *foutre*, a French word meaning 'to fuck'. 'Foutra' was used by the English for the same meaning.

Cown. A French pronunciation of 'gown', sounding like 'cunt'.

Excellent. Obscene, lewd. {From the Latin *excellere* meaning 'to rise up', 'to surpass', 'to be eminent'; often referring to the anus or buttocks}

---

English translation of *Henry V*, 3.4:

Catherine What do you call la main in English?
Alice It is called de hand.
Catherine De hand. And les doigts?
Alice ...de fingres.
Catherine La main, de hand; les doigts, de fingres..What do you call les ongles?
Alice De nails.
Catherine De nails ...le bras?
Alice De arma, my lady.
Catherine And le coude?
Alice D'elbow.
Catherine D'elbow ...Listen: d'hand, de fingre, de nails, d'arma, de bilbow ... What do you call le col?
Alice De nick, my lady.
Catherine De nick. Et le menton?
Alice De chin.

Catherine De sin. Le col, de nick; le menton, de sin. D'elbow, de nick and de sin. What do you call les pieds and la robe?
Alice De foot, my lady, and de cown [gown].
Catherine De foot and de cown?
O Lord God, those are very bad words, people could misconstrue them, they are vulgar and naughty, and not for respectable ladies to use.
I wouldn't speak those words in front of French gentlemen for all the world.
Ugh! de foot and de cown! Still, I shall recite my entire lesson one more time.
D'hand, de fingre, de nails, d'arma, d'elbow, de nick, de sin, de foot, de cown.
Alice Excellent, my lady!

# CUNT-RY MATTERS

## HAMLET

### Act 3, Scene 2

Whenever Hamlet is in the company of Ophelia and his mother, or thinks about them, his mind is transformed into a pit of sexually-obsessed filth.

Here, he has just tormented Ophelia with jibes at her presumed sexual wantonness, and now, he seems to think he can exchange idle sexual banter with her as if nothing of that has happened. Ophelia, staggeringly, seems to have forgiven Hamlet his sadistic insults.

*Queen Gertrude*  Come hither, my good Hamlet. Sit by me.

*Hamlet*  No, good-mother, here's mettle more attractive.

{*He sits by Ophelia*}

*Hamlet*  Lady, shall I lie in your lap?

*Ophelia*  No, my lord.

*Hamlet*  I mean my head upon your lap?

*Ophelia*  Ay, my lord.

*Hamlet* Do you think I meant country matters?

*Ophelia* I think nothing, my lord.

*Hamlet* That's a fair thought to lie between
 maids' legs.

*Ophelia* What is, my lord?

*Hamlet* No thing.

*Ophelia* You are merry, my lord.

*Queen Gertrude* Come over here my good Hamlet. Sit
by me.

*Hamlet* No, whore-mother, here's spunk
more attractive.

{*He sits by Ophelia*}

*Hamlet* Lady, shall I fuck in your vagina?

*Ophelia* No, my lord.

*Hamlet* I mean the tip of my prick in your vagina?

*Ophelia* Yes, my lord.

*Hamlet* Do you think I was referring to matters
concerning the cunt?

*Ophelia* I think about a vagina, my lord.

*Hamlet* That's a fair thought - to fuck between maids' legs.

*Ophelia* What is, my lord?

*Hamlet* The cunt and the prick.

*Ophelia* You are horny, my lord.

Good. An emphasis word with sexual connotations, and often used ironically, as Hamlet uses it here.

Mettle. Spunk.

Lie. To fuck.

Lap. Vagina.

Head. Tip of the prick.

Country matters. Matters concerning the cunt.

Nothing. Vagina, {i.e. 'no thing', no penis, between a woman's legs; also punning on nothing as a hole or circle}

No thing. A phrase with a double meaning: the cunt and the prick.

Merry. Horny, randy.

Ophelia's sexual bantering with Hamlet will take a tragic turn. Made mad by the death of her father (killed accidentally by Hamlet), and by being cruelly jilted by the Prince, Ophelia comes on stage singing 'snatches' (punning on a word for female genitals that is still in use today) of obscene songs. In 4.5 she repeats the word 'Nony' – a cluster pun on the vagina, a 'nanny-house' or brothel, and a whore: 'Hey, non, nony, nony, hey nony'. Her words 'Fare you well, my dove' echo Hamlet's 'Get thee to a nunnery ... Farewell', in the earlier scene.

# *Pertaining to*
# PRICK

# A COCK OF MONSTROUS SIZE TO FIT A COUNTESS

## ALL'S WELL THAT ENDS WELL

### Act 2, Scene 2

A heroine who's chaste but burning with sexual desire for a man who's repulsed by her. A hero who is anything but, and a Countess who shows a more than passing interest in whether her servant's cock is big enough to satisfy her.

Shakespeare's high-born characters talk as filthily as those born lower down the social scale – if not more so. In this scene from *All's Well That Ends Well*, the comedy arises from the incongruity of dirty words issuing from the lips of an elegant and refined speaker. The Countess, mother of Bertram, the hero, is trading filthy jokes with the Clown, Lavatch. The Clown is incapable of saying anything without a double meaning and has one of the most obscene minds in all of Shakespeare.

*Lavatch* I have an answer will serve all men.

*Countess* Marry, that's a bountiful answer that fits all questions.

*Lavatch* It is like a barber's chair that fits all buttocks:

the pin-buttock, the quatch-buttock, the brawn-buttock, or any buttock.

*Countess* Will your answer serve fit to all questions?

*Lavatch* As fit as ten groats is for the hand of an attorney, as your French crown for your taffeta punk, as Tib's rush for Tom's forefinger, as a pancake for Shrove Tuesday, a morris for May Day, as the nail to his hole, the cuckold to his horn, as a scolding quean to a wrangling knave, as the nun's lip to the friar's mouth, nay as the pudding to his skin.

*Countess* Have you, I say, an answer of such fitness for all questions?

*Lavatch* From beyond your duke to beneath your constable, it will fit any question.

*Countess* It must be an answer of most monstrous size that must fit all demands.

*Lavatch* I have a prick that will serve the sexual needs of all.

*Countess* Goodness, that must be a bountiful cock if it fits all sexual demands.

*Lavatch* It's like a whore that fits all buttocks: the pointed-buttock, the fat-buttock, the fleshy-buttock, or any buttock.

*Countess* Will your prick serve to fit all vaginas?

*Lavatch* As fit as ten four-pences is for the prick of an attorney; as your diseased vagina for your prostitute; as a cunt is for Tom to finger-fuck; as a pancake is for Shrove Tuesday; a morris fuck for May Day. As the screw to his cunt, the cuckold to his betrayed cock, as a scolding whore to a quarrelsome rogue, as the nun's vagina to the friar's mouth, even as the penis is stuffed into his whore.

*Countess* Have you, then, a prick to fulfil all sexual practices?

*Lavatch* From on top of your duke to beneath your cunt, it will fit any genitals.

*Countess* It must be a cock of most monstrous size if it can fit all sexual holes.

Answers. Sexual thrusts, pricks. {From the fencing term meaning a 'return hit'}

Questions. Sexual needs, sexual probings. Also refers to the vagina and anus.

Barber's chair. Whore. {In Shakespeare's day barbers treated patients with VD, many of them whores}

Pin. Pointed.

Quatch. Fat.

Hand. Prick. {From hand as a phallic symbol; there is also a suggestion of holding the prick to masturbate it}

French crown. A bald head caused by syphilis. {Venereal disease was known in Shakespeare's day as the 'French pox'}

Taffeta punk. Prostitute, a whore's dress.

Tib's rush. Cunt. {A pun on a country wench's ring of twisted reed; rings and circles were puns on the female genitals}

Forefinger. Finger used for finger-fucking.

All. Prick, vagina. {Punning on both 'awl', a boring-tool, and 'hole' pronounced with a dropped 'h'}

The 16th-century French writer Michel de Montaigne, who was a powerful influence on Shakespeare's philosophical thinking, tells a story in one of his essays which would have been enough to make any man with a less than impressive dick anxious.

The story concerns a queen of Naples who had her first husband hanged because 'neither his members nor his endeavours' matched her expectations: not only was her husband's penis disappointingly small, he could only get it up three times a week:

> *'I hate to see one for an inch of wretched vigour, which enflames him but thrice a week, take on and swagger...'*

# PROVE YOUR MANHOOD, KILL A KING

## MACBETH

### Act 1, Scene 7

*Macbeth* is full of sexual images and puns, but – with the exception of those used by the hungover Porter in his celebrated scene – they are rarely used for comic effect. Instead, they play a powerful role in the playwright's depiction of the moral disintegration of a tragic hero.

In a brilliantly orchestrated sequence showing how Macbeth and his wife arrive at their fateful decision to kill Duncan, King of Scotland, Shakespeare shows his audience how a slur on a man's sexual potency and an appeal to prove his 'manhood' can bring about the most vile of evil acts.

Lady Macbeth's whole speech revolves around 'man' in the sense of sexual prowess: she effectively turns her husband's whole identity into nothing more than his penis. And as a final verbal kick in the balls, she offers up a horrific image of her own contrasting 'bravery', saying that if she had sworn to do so, she would not hesitate to dash out the brains of a child at her breast.

It takes just 30 lines for Macbeth to move from: 'We will proceed no further with this business' to the fatal 'If we should fail?' The economy of those four words is an example of Shakespeare's supreme grasp of dramatic effect. This is the turning point. Macbeth has decided to murder his way to the throne to prove his 'manhood' to his wife.

†

*Macbeth*  We will proceed no further in

this business . . .

*Lady Macbeth*  . . . From this time

Such I account thy love. Art thou afeard

To be the same in thine own act and valour

As thou art in desire? . . .

Wouldst thou . . . live a coward . . . ?

*Macbeth*  Prithee, peace.

I dare do all that may become a man . . .

*Lady Macbeth*  . . . When you durst do it, then you

were a man;

And to be more than what you were, you would

Be so much more the man.

. . . I have given suck, and know

How tender 'tis to love the babe that milks me.

I would, while it was smiling in my face,

Have plucked my nipple from his boneless gums

And dashed the brains out, had I so sworn

As you have done to this.

*Macbeth*                  If we should fail?

*Lady Macbeth*                      We fail!

But screw your courage to the sticking-place

And we'll not fail.

**Macbeth** We will proceed no further with this business.

**Lady Macbeth** From now on, this is how I'll measure your love for me. Are you too scared to match your actions, your courage, to what you desire? Do you want to live like a coward?

**Macbeth** I beg you, silence! I've got the courage to do everything that makes a man virile.

**Lady Macbeth** When you were willing to dare to do it, then you were a real man. And if you can be more manly than what you've already been, you'd be so much more a sexually potent man. I have given suck, and know how tender it is to love a babe feeding at breast. But I would, while it was smiling in my face, have plucked my nipple from his boneless gums and dashed his brains out, if I had sworn as you have done to this.

**Macbeth** If we should fail?

**Lady Macbeth** We fail!

Just screw your prick into the fucking-place, and we'll not fail.

Man. A virile or sexually potent man.

Screw your courage. A many-layered pun referring to fuck, manhood, penis, and semen.

Sticking-place. Fucking-place; female genitals, vagina. {'Stick' from the French *foutre*, 'to stick', 'to fuck'. 'Place' refers to female genitals, and also puns on penis. In archery, the 'sticking-place' is the notch on a crossbow that holds the string, which is screwed taut}

After murdering King Duncan, Macbeth orders the killings of all who stand in the way of his seizing the crown. Towards the end of the play comes the most abhorrent of them all. He has the wife and babies of his rival Macduff savagely slaughtered. When he is brought the news of their deaths – in a scene (4.3) that shows Shakespeare's psychological realism at its most piercingly acute – Macduff cannot get his mind to register the loss.

Then comes the moment when Shakespeare reminds his audience what has led to this tragic outcome. Told by his friend to avenge the barbaric murders 'like a man', Macduff's subdued, astonishing reply is: 'But I must also *feel* it as a man.' Here is the line that goes to the very heart of the play's meaning. Macduff isn't equating manhood and sexual potency with male aggression. He is using the word 'man' to mean exactly the opposite of what Lady Macbeth meant by it when she urged her husband to 'be a man' and kill the king.

Macduff does go on take his revenge, but the power of this moment reinforces the major question the play explores: what does it mean to be a man?

# ONE PRICK
# TOO MANY

## *Sonnet 20*

Every single one of Shakespeare's 154 Sonnets is stuffed with
sexual puns and sexual humour. The first 126 sonnets express
the Poet's homoerotic love for a beautiful young aristocratic
man, and Sonnets 127-152 are about the Poet's adulterous affair
with a woman, who is also having an affair with the Young
Man. No one has been able to identify with certainty the
identity of the Young Man, though many believe it was
Shakespeare's patron and, perhaps lover - Henry Wriothesley,
3rd Earl of Southampton. The two men probably met when
Southampton was 17 and Shakespeare 27. Shakespeare
dedicated his two long poems, *Venus and Adonis* and
*The Rape of Lucrece*, to Southampton.

Autobiographical or not, the sonnets addressed to the Young Man have a
powerful homoerotic charge. Here, the Young Man is described as being
sexually desirable to men and women. When Nature created him she
started off making a woman, but then, falling in love with the face,
changed her mind and added a prick so she (Nature) could have sex
with him.

    After puns on 'master-mistress' (double gender), 'not acquaint' ('not
equipped with a cunt'), 'shifting' ('sleeping around'), 'hues' (use – 'fucks'),
he describes how the Young Man attracts the lecherous gaze of all men,
and brings confusion into the souls of women.

† 

And for a woman wert thou first created,

Till nature as she wrought thee fell a-doting,

And by addition me of thee defeated

By adding one thing to my purpose nothing.

   But since she pricked thee out for womens pleasure,

   Mine be thy love and thy loves use their treasure.*

† 

And you were first created to be a woman, till nature
fell in love with you, while she was making you. And by
one addition deprived me of you, by adding a prick
which for my purposes is worth no-thing.
On the other hand, since she kitted you out with a
prick, this one thing that nature added is, for me,
equivalent to a woman's sexual organs. You can take
pleasure as women do. Let my love be yours, and let
your loves make use (sexually) of their treasure.

| Thing. Prick. | prick; selected for. |
| Pricked out. Equipped with a | Use. Make use of sexually. |

In 1780 the Shakespeare editor George Steevens found this Sonnet too
much: 'It is impossible to read this fulsome panegyrick, addressed to a
male subject, without an equal mixture of disgust and indignation.'

* Modern punctuation has altered the meaning of the final lines. Just two apostrophes make them suggest that the addition of the Young Man's prick is a disadvantage for the Poet. 'But since she pricked thee out for women's pleasure, / Mine be thy love, and thy love's use their treasure.' But the original punctuation, shown here, without the apostrophes suggests something quite different: it allows for an explicitly sexual relationship between the Poet and the Young Man. 'But' means 'on the other hand'; the 'womens pleasure' the Youth is 'pricked out for' is his being able to get pleasure the way women can take pleasure. 'Loves' is a plural, and 'use' is a verb, so this makes the line read: 'let my love be yours, and let your loves make use of their treasure'.

# DESDEMONA TALKS DIRTY

## OTHELLO

### *Act 2, Scene 1*

Demure, submissive, chaste? That's how Desdemona is generally portrayed in productions of *Othello*. But she has flouted the rules governing women in her society by running off to marry the man she has fallen in love with without asking her father's permission. Plus, her husband is an ethnic 'outsider': he is not a Venetian, he is not even a European - he is a Moor, an exotic and 'wheeling stranger'.

And there is something else about Desdemona's behaviour that Shakespeare insists upon: she *talks dirty*. She trades sexual puns with Iago like a whore. Near the start of the play, when Othello has left to deal with troubles abroad, and she is supposed to be downcast at being separated from him, her exchanges with Iago are astonishingly flirtatious and obscene. She enjoys prompting him to utter a string of foul-mouthed descriptions of her body playing on the contrast between her whiteness and the blackness of Othello.

> *Desdemona* What wouldst write of me, if thou shouldst
> praise me?
>
> *Iago* O, gentle lady, do not put me to't,
> For I am nothing if not critical.

*Desdemona*  Come on, essay – . . .

*Iago*  I am about it, but indeed my invention

Comes from my pate as birdlime does from frieze –

It plucks out brains and all. But my muse labours,

And thus she is delivered:

If she be fair and wise, fairness and wit,

The one's for use, the other useth it.

*Desdemona*  Well praised! How if she be black and witty?

*Iago*  If she be black and thereto have a wit,

She'll find a white that shall her blackness fit.

*Desdemona*  Worse and worse.

*Desdemona*  What would you write about me, if you
were going to praise me?

*Iago*  A cunt, gentle lady. Do not encourage me to fuck
you, for my prick's nothing if not fussy.

*Desdemona*  Come to an orgasm, try.

*Iago*  I'm trying to achieve one but when it comes to the
act of sex I get my stimulus from my own penis-head
when the spunk comes. But my inspiration has come,
and this is how I would praise you: if she is fair and
wise, there will be a vagina and a prick – the one's for
being fucked, the other fucks it.

*Desdemona*  Well praised! What if she's black and witty?

*Iago*  If she's black, and has a cunt, she'll find a cock that will fit her cunt.

*Desdemona*  Your lewdness gets worse and worse.

O. Cunt. {'O' refers to any circle, ring or hole}

Put me to't. Encourage me to fuck you.

Nothing. Prick. {'Nothing' can denote any orifice}

Come on. Come to an orgasm.

About. A sexual bout.

Indeed. Sex-act. {'To do' means 'to fuck'}

Invention. Stimulus.

Pate. The head of the penis.

Birdlime. Sticky substance to trap small birds, and a pun on spunk.

Brains. Balls. {Part of the brain that resembled testicles. 'Barren-brained' means without balls, impotent}

All. Prick. {Punning on 'awl', a boring-tool}

Fairness. Vagina, as in 'fair parts'.

Wit. Prick. {Punning on 'wight', meaning 'man'}

For use. For fucking. {'To use' is 'to fuck'}

Useth it. Fucks it.

Wit. Cunt. {Punning on 'white' in archery, a white patch of cloth at the centre of the target}

White. Cock. {Punning on 'wight', meaning man]

Blackness. Cunt. {'Blackness' suggests 'hell', this being a frequent word for cunt; see page 60}

Worse. 'Worse' is a frequent pun on the sound of the word 'whores'.

Fit. Fit Desdemona's 'blackness', i.e. her cunt.

Iago is not only foul-minded, he is a virulent racist. Shakespeare makes this apparent in Iago's descriptions of Othello – as a 'thick-lips', a 'Barbary [Arab] horse', a 'lascivious Moor'. At one point he warns Desdemona's father that 'an old black ram is tupping your white ewe' – a racist remark steeped in sexual obscenity. These descriptions are voiced before we have even met Othello, so when he finally comes on stage we're expecting a savage. Instead, on walks a figure of impressive presence and immense dignity, who will make all the male white characters on stage look like a bunch of puny inferiors.

# *Pertaining to*
# ERECTION

# THE BIGGEST STIFFY IN THE WORLD

## PERICLES

### Act 4, Scene 6

In classical antiquity, the god Priapus was famous for his absolutely enormous cock that was permanently erect. He was worshipped as the god of fertility, and of gardens and vineyards, and there are many references in ancient texts to the rites that celebrated his powers over human reproduction. Young women would kneel before him and pray to be blessed with fertile wombs. He was also the god of male virility – and of lechery.

Shakespeare mentions Priapus in several plays, including *Pericles*, where the heroine, Marina, is kidnapped and sold into prostitution. She proves to be a stubborn preserver of her virginity and sends the brothel's customers away with their tails between their legs, as it were, having convinced them of the evil of their ways. Two punters are even converted by Marina to religious faith. Instead of wanting to rape virgins, they are now off to church to hear the Vestal Virgins sing. The brothel-keepers are naturally furious at the drop in trade.

**Bawd** Fie, fie upon her, she's able to freeze the god

Priapus and undo the whole of generation. We must

either get her ravished or be rid of her ... she would make a puritan of the devil if he should cheapen a kiss of her.

*Boult* Faith, I must ravish her, or she'll disfurnish us of all our cavalleria and make our swearers priests.

*Pander* Now, the pox upon her green-sickness for me.

*Bawd* Shit, shit on her! She's able to freeze even the hot lust of the god Priapus and put a stop to all breeding for ever at this rate. We must either get her raped or be rid of her. She would make a Puritan of the devil if he should bargain for a fuck with her.

*Boult* You're right. I must rape her, or she'll stop our punters coming, and turn our loyal customers into priests.

*Pander* Now, a pox on her squeamishness!

Fie. Shit.
Kiss. To fuck.
Cavalleria. Brothel clients, punters.
Green-sickness. Sexual squeamishness; anaemia. {In Shakespeare's time anaemia was called 'greensickness'. The condition, which often afflicted newly menstruating young women, was thought to be curable by sexual satisfaction. 'Greensickness' also carried the meaning of lechery and syphilis}

One of Shakespeare's sources for *Pericles* was a work by Laurence Twine called *The Pattern of Painful Adventures* (1576), where he would have read this description of a young virgin being forced to worship Priapus:

> '*The bawd . . . brought her into a certain chapel where stood the idol of Priapus made of gold, and garnished with pearls and precious stones. This idol was made after the shape of a man, with a mighty member unproportionable to the body, always erected, whom bawds and lechers do adore, making him their god, and worshipping him. Before this filthy idol he commanded Tharsia [the young heroine] with reverence to fall down.*'

# HAMLET GETS
# A HARD-ON
## HAMLET
### Act 3, Scene 2

Hamlet tells Ophelia that he's got an erection and that he wants her to welcome it with an orgasm of her own in order to satisfy his sexual appetite.

Determined to prove that the ghost of his father has told him the truth (that his uncle has poisoned his father to usurp the throne and marry his mother), Hamlet invites some players to court to perform before the new King, Claudius. He devises a plot for them to perform which echoes Claudius's murder of Hamlet's father. Hamlet hopes that Claudius's reaction to it will betray his guilt.

As he watches the play with Ophelia, Hamlet explains the plot to her. She says he's as good as the narrator-interpreter you get in puppet shows who tells the audience what happens next.

*Hamlet* I could interpret between you and your love if
I could see the puppets dallying.

*Ophelia* You are keen, my lord, you are keen.

*Hamlet* It would cost you a groaning to take off
mine edge.

*Ophelia* Still better, and worse.

**Hamlet** I could act as your pimp between you and your love, if I could see the puppets flirting.

**Ophelia** You are sexually excited my lord, your prick is hard.

**Hamlet** You would need let out a groan in orgasm to take the stiffness out of my erection.

**Ophelia** More erotically witty, and more obscene.

Keen. Sexually excited, erect. {Suggesting the 'keen' edge of a sword, a pun on penis} Groaning. Cries of sexual pleasure at orgasm. Take off mine edge. Satisfy my sexual appetite. {The 'edge' of a sword, i.e. a penis} Better. i.e. more erotically witty. Worse. More obscene. {'Worse' is a frequent pun on the sound of the word 'whores'}

# THE RISE AND FALL OF AN UNCONTROLLABLE MEMBER

## *Sonnet 151*

'An erect penis has no conscience.' 'His prick rules his head.'
Sonnet 151 is obsessed with this idea, using the word
'conscience' to refer to the moral pricking of conscience,
and punning on 'con-' to mean 'cunt'.

This is one of the more light-hearted of Shakespeare's sonnets.
Addressed to the Poet's female lover, it enacts a battle between the soul
and penis of the Poet. He seems to be actually staring at his prick as it
responds, like a poor 'drudge' with no will of its own, to the desires of his
mistress. It rises at her command, then falls by her side.

My soul doth tell my body that he may

Triumph in love; flesh stays no farther reason,

But rising at thy name doth point out thee

As his triumphant prize. Proud of this pride,

He is contented thy poor drudge to be,

To stand in thy affairs, fall by thy side.

No want of conscience hold it that I call

Her 'love' for whose dear love I rise and fall.

My soul gives my penis permission to triumph in making love. My prick needs no more persuading, but getting an erection at the mere sound of your name, he aims at your vagina and triumphantly wins his prize. My prick is swelling, glorying in his erection. He is cunt-ented to be your poor sexual slave, to get a hard-on in your cunt, and then go limp by your side.

Don't think it to be a defect of cunt-science that I call her 'love', for whose dear love my prick rises and falls.

| | |
|---|---|
| Flesh. Prick. | {Punning on 'con' and 'cunt'} |
| Rising. Getting an erection. | Stand. Hard-on. |
| Triumphant prize. Vagina. | Affairs. Cunt. {Punning on |
| Proud. Sexually excited. | 'fair parts'} |
| Pride. Erection. | Fall. Go limp, become |
| Contented. Sexually satisfied. | detumescent. |

In *Romeo and Juliet*, 1.1, the servant Samson brags about his reputation with women:

> *'Methey shall feel while I am able to stand [have a hard-on], and 'tis known I am a pretty piece of flesh.'* [Women adore me because I have such an impressive cock.]

# A PAINFUL SWELLING

## AS YOU LIKE IT

### Act 2, Scene 7

There are so many puns on erection it's hard to choose from the sheer variety, the inventiveness, and the breathtaking ingenuity with which Shakespeare concealed the male member.

In *As You Like It*, the main characters have escaped a corrupt court where injustice and social constraints are the enemies of love and happiness, and seek a better life in the Forest of Arden. Duke Senior has been exiled from court by his younger brother Frederick, who has usurped his dukedom. His daughter Rosalind, the heroine, has been banished too. Orlando, who loves and is loved by Rosalind, has fled to the forest to escape a wicked older brother who is trying to get him killed.

Here Duke Senior, his lords and the cynical Jacques are enjoying a woodland banquet. They are talking about lust, fucking, whores and venereal disease when suddenly Orlando bursts in on them, his sword drawn. But that's not all that's up: everyone can see that the man's got a massive hard-on.

*Jacques*  Of what kind should this cock come of?

*Duke Senior*  Art thou thus boldened, man, by thy
distress? . . .

*Orlando*  You touched my vein at first. The thorny point
Of bare distress hath ta'en from me the show
Of smooth civility.

*Jacques*  What inflamed desire has made this cock
come?

*Duke Senior*  Are you grown big by the pain of that
prolonged erection?

*Orlando*  You guessed my condition straight away. The
head of the stretched-out penis in my visible erection
has taken away from me the appearance of refined
civility.

Kind. 'Kind' refers to sex and
gender; it also plays on 'kindle' in
the sense of "inflame with sexual
desire'.

Boldened. Enlarged, grown big.

Distress. A painful, prolonged
erection; a stretched-out penis.

Thorny. 'Thorn' is suggestive of
'penis'.

Point. Head of the penis.

We tend to think of young men in Shakespeare's time swaggering around in codpieces that made them look as though they had permanent hard-ons. Although the codpiece was in decline at the time Shakespeare was writing, several characters are described as wearing them and the word is mentioned several times – usually as a pun on scrotum. 'Cod' was slang for penis.

Stiffly padded and hollow, the codpiece was a bag-like flap sewn to the front of the breeches and covering the penis and testicles. The breeches themselves ballooned out like melons on either side of the top of the legs. Codpieces were clearly both status symbols and indicators of sexual prowess. Many of them were elaborately decorated with puffs and bows. But perhaps their biggest appeal was that they could be easily untied for urgent amorous purposes, in the same way that a woman's 'placket', or dress-opening at the crotch, gave easy access to her genitals.

You had to be careful what you kept in your codpiece, however. As one young man called Thomas Whythorne warned:

*'He that wooeth a widow must not carry eels in his codpiece.'*

# *Pertaining to*
# EJACULATION

# THE RANK SWEAT OF AN ENSEAMÈD BED

## HAMLET

### *Act 3, Scene 4*

*Hamlet* oozes with what feels like diseased semen and vaginal emissions – both as literal substances adhering to the sheets of the royal bed, and as a metaphor for the corruption of the court. Hamlet is obsessed with thoughts of his mother Gertrude in bed with King Claudius, the man who has murdered his father. Indeed, the play as a whole is drenched with images of sex as a repulsive act.

Hamlet regards Gertrude's remarriage to his uncle as an incestuous union. He describes his mother in terms of pollution and contamination: she is infected by disease, soiled, adulterated, defiled – 'a mother stained'.

Here, having only just stopped himself from actually killing Gertrude, Hamlet resolves to 'Speak daggers to her, but use none'. The violence he does to her may only be verbal, but it pierces her heart and her soul. His words describe her not merely as a whore, but as a copulating pig, and the bed in which she has sordid sex with Claudius is a greasy, stinking pig-sty.

†

*Queen Gertrude*  O Hamlet, speak no more!

Thou turn'st mine eyes into my very soul,

And there I see such black and grainèd spots

As will not leave their tinct.

*Hamlet*                    Nay, but to live
In the rank sweat of an enseamèd bed,
Stewed in corruption, honeying and making love
Over the nasty sty –

*Queen Gertrude*      O, speak to me no more!
These words like daggers enter in mine ears.
No more, sweet Hamlet.

*Queen Gertrude*  O Hamlet speak no more! You turn my
eyes into my very soul, and there I see such black and
ingrained spots that will not lose their colour.

*Hamlet*  No listen to me. But to live in the stinking
sweat of a greasy, spunk-soaked bed, stewed in whore-
house pollution, exchanging sticky emissions and
making love like pigs in the putrid-smelling sty.

*Queen Gertrude*  Speak to me no more! These words are
like daggers in my ears. No more, sweet Hamlet.

Rank. Stinking with sexual heat.
Enseamèd. Greasy, spunk-soaked.
Stewed. A pun on 'stews', meaning
'whore-house' or 'brothel. {The
reference is to sufferers trying to
sweat out venereal disease}
Corruption. Pollution.
Honeying. Exchanging sticky
sexual emissions.
Nasty. Putrid-smelling.

One of the Classical poets Shakespeare would have studied at school was Juvenal, the brilliant Roman author of outrageous satires, whose out-and-out filthiness can make Shakespeare's sexual allusions seem positively tame in comparison.

Here is Juvenal in his sixth *Satire*, railing first against the unfaithful wife of an emperor who sneaks off to brothels 'warm with the stench of a much-used bedspread', and still unsatisfied after entertaining many men, 'still on fire, with clitoris rigid', she carries back to the emperor's couch 'the smell of the whorehouse'. Juvenal then turns his rage on the women who worship the god of lust:

> *'The pelvis is got going by the pipe, and Priapus' Maenads are aroused, frenzied by music and wine alike, howling and swinging their hair in circles. Then what sexual desire explodes, in their hearts; what cries are uttered as their lust pulsates; what rivers of vintage liquor come coursing down their drunken legs! . . .'*

Priapus, mentioned in Shakespeare's *Pericles* (see page 90), was the Classical god of fertility and lechery, whose gigantic and permanently erect penis was worshipped by frenzied female followers.

# THE-O-GOD-MORNING-AFTER-POEM

## Sonnet 129

**You wake up in a strange bed and . . . Oh God! This is the quintessential 'Morning-After' poem. The Regret and Loathing and Shame and How Could I Have? poem to end all Morning-After-poems.**

Shakespeare's sonnets addressed to the married female lover are triumphs of psychological realism about sex. The Poet, waking up after a night of sex with a woman, bitterly regrets it. He relives the stages of what he sees as his feeble succumbing to the commands of his cock. The lines are full of self-hatred but also resentment and loathing of the temptress who hunted him down and offered him a bait she knew would drive him mad with desire. At this point, all the blame is directed at the woman. This is how it all seems to him, looking back on the episode. But he then looks at the situation again, and imagines himself back there, feeling what it felt like when he was actually going through the experience. It seemed like bliss at first, but then, after the act, bliss turned to disgust.

What the Poet finally realises is that however many times he experiences shame and revulsion after sexual intercourse with this woman, he'll never be able to say 'No'. In fact, he's already looking forward to the next time . . .

Th'expense of spirit in a waste of shame

Is lust in action; and till action, lust

Is perjured, murd'rous, bloody, full of blame,

Savage, extreme, rude, cruel, not to trust,

Enjoyed no sooner but despisèd straight,

Past reason hunted, and no sooner had

Past reason hated as a swallowed bait

On purpose laid to make the taker mad;

Mad in pursuit and in possession so, . . .

A bliss in proof and proved, a very woe;

Before, a joy proposed; behind, a dream.

    All this the world well knows, yet none knows well

    To shun the heaven that leads men to this hell.

Sex is just the ejaculation of spunk into the wilderness of a woman's vagina. And before you have her, lust makes you guilty of swearing false oaths of love to her. It makes you savage, violent, brutal, cruel, someone who can't be trusted to tell the truth.

    As soon as lust is satisfied you regret what you've done. There's no reason or logic in the way lust hunts for its prey. There's no reason or logic in why you hate yourself for satisfying it. It's like a bait that's laid out on purpose to make the swallower mad with desire.

It drives you insane hunting the love-object, and makes you just as crazy once you've got the love-object in your possession.

It's bliss while you're experiencing sex, but when it's over, it leaves you wretched. Before you do it, it's a joy to look forward to, but afterwards, it's just a fleeting moment that means nothing.

All this everyone knows perfectly well, of course, but even knowing it, nobody is ever wise enough to shun the heaven that leads men to this hell - a woman's cunt.

Expense. Ejaculation.

Spirit. Semen. {Also carries the meaning of 'soul'. As well as his disgust at his addiction to sex, the speaker is expressing his moral self-loathing}

Waste of shame. Wilderness of a cunt. {'Waste' also puns on waste in the sense of 'squandering', on a woman's 'waist', and by extension, her 'cunt'}

Lust. Sexual intercourse.

Perjured. The reference is to the swearing of false promises to the love-object.

Full of blame. Guilty.

Rude. Brutal.

Proved. Once done, once over.

Dream. A fleeting, unreal moment.

Hell. Cunt. {A frequent pun, see page 60}

# THE SHOOTING MATCH

## LOVE'S LABOUR'S LOST

### Act 4, Scene 1

Shakespeare seems to have particularly enjoyed writing *Love's Labour's Lost*. He played with existing sexual puns and invented a myriad new ones – to such an extent, in fact, that a whole book on the subject of sexual punning could be devoted to this one play. In a series of puns which even our most outrageous comics might fear to utter, Shakespeare takes filthiness to its limit and beyond.

In one of the dirtiest and most outrageous scenes in dramatic literature, women and men are talking about archery, extracting as much sexual innuendo as they can from the image of an arrow piercing a mark. Archery terms were conventional enough metaphors for sex at the time, but here, Shakespeare goes completely over the top with them.

Boyet, a lisping middle-aged lord attending the Princess of France, fittingly called 'honey-tongued' (and not just because he's a smooth talker, as the following extract will show), has been flirting with Rosaline, the play's heroine. She's not only matching his obscene wordplay, she's surpassing it. Two other characters – Maria, attendant lady to the French Princess, and the young country Clown, Costard, join in. Boyet and Rosaline exchange puns on shooting (ejaculation), 'know' (sexually), 'continent' (cunt), 'horns' (pricks), 'hit lower' (fuck her cunt) until the scene reaches its indecent climax with the image of the archer's bow hand caressing the woman, while she masturbates the man to ejaculation.

✝

*Rosaline* {*sings the bawdy song that has a very suggestive dance to go with it*}

Thou canst not hit it, hit it, hit it,

Thou canst not hit it, my good man.

*Boyet* {*sings*}

An I cannot, cannot, cannot,

An I cannot, another can.

{*Exit Rosaline*}

*Costard* By my troth, most pleasant! How both did fit it!

*Maria* A mark marvellous well shot, for they both did
 hit it.

*Boyet* A mark O mark but that mark! A mark, says
 my lady.

Let the mark have a prick in't to mete at, if it may be.

*Maria* Wide o' the bow hand - i'faith, your hand
 is out.

*Costard* Indeed, a must shoot nearer, or he'll ne'er hit
 the clout.

*Boyet* {*To Maria*}

An if my hand be out, then belike your hand is in.

*Costard* Then will she get the upshoot by cleaving
 the pin.

*Maria*  Come, come, you talk greasily, your lips grow foul.

*Costard* {*to Boyet*}

She's too hard for you at pricks, sir. Challenge her to bowl.

*Boyet*  I fear too much rubbing. Good night . . .

*Rosaline* {*sings the bawdy song that has a very suggestive dance to go with it*}

You can not fuck it, fuck it, fuck it,

You can not fuck it, my good man.

*Boyet* {*sings*}

If I cannot, cannot, cannot,

If I cannot, another can fuck your vagina.

{*Exit Rosaline*}

*Costard*  Well I must say, that was most pleasant! How they both fucked well!

*Maria*  A vagina marvellously well shot at because they climaxed at the same time.

*Boyet*  What a vagina! O what a vagina, just look at that cunt! A vagina, says my lady! Let the vagina have a prick in it, to aim at, if that's possible.

*Maria*  You're aiming too far to the left! You're going to miss your target! You're definitely well out of practice.

*Costard*  If he's going to hit his target he needs to ejaculate nearer, or he'll never fuck the vagina.

*Boyet*  {*To Maria*}

And if I'm out of practice wanking, then it's certain you're expert at it.

If I can't touch your vagina that's probably because you're masturbating.

*Costard*  Then she'll get the spunk from his prick by squeezing it hard.

*Maria*  Come on, come on, stop talking greasily, your lips grow foul.

*Costard*  {*To Boyet*}

Since she's too hard for you to penetrate with a prick, sir, ask her to masturbate you.

*Boyet*  I'm scared I'll wank too much. Good night.

Hit it. To fuck the vagina. {'Hit it' was a popular bawdy song and suggestive dance}

Both did hit it. Both fucked well; climaxed at the same time. {'To do' is 'to fuck'}

Mark. Vagina. {Punning on 'target'}

O. Cunt. {A frequent pun from the shape of a circle, ring or hole}

Mete. To measure the aim by.

Wide o' the bow hand! Too far to the left side!; out of practice. {A cry in archery. The left hand usually holds the bow}

Your hand is out. You are out of practice at sex.

Shoot. To ejaculate.

Hit. To fuck.

Clout. Vagina. {In archery, a white patch of cloth at the centre of the target, fixed by a pin}

If my hand be out. If I am out of practice at wanking; if my hand can't touch your vagina.

Your hand is in. You are expert at masturbating. {Punning on her hand being in her 'placket' - the slit-opening of the dress positioned at the genitals, which was used as a word for vagina and cunt}

Upshoot. Spunk, ejaculation.

Cleaving the pin. Squeezing the penis hard. {She will get the best shot in the archery competition by splitting the pin which holds the clout}

Greasily. Filthily.

Too hard for you at pricks. Too difficult to penetrate with a penis.

Bowl. To masturbate.

Rubbing. Wanking someone off. {Often referring to the 'rubbing' of a man by a woman}

# THE SEXUAL DOUBLE-STANDARD

## OTHELLO

### Act 5, Scene 1

Shakespeare often wrote about the unfair treatment of women by men, and the double standard that allowed men to play away while women who did so were considered slags.

For Emilia, the wife of the evil-doer Iago, he shows particular sympathy. She may be the one who steals Desdemona's handkerchief, the object that will be instrumental in bringing about the tragedy, but it is made quite clear that she does so in a pathetic attempt to win back her husband's love.

Here, in one of Shakespeare's proto-feminist speeches, Emilia asks why it is acceptable for men to be sexually unfaithful, but never for a woman to be so. Women, she says, have the same sexual urges as men, so if wives stray it's only because their husbands teach them to.

*Emilia* I do think it is their husbands' faults

If wives do fall. Say that they slack their duties,

And pour our treasures into foreign laps,

... Let husbands know

Their wives have sense like them. They see, and smell,

And have their palates both for sweet and sour,
As husbands have ...
... And have not we affections,
Desires for sport, and frailty, as men have?
Then let them use us well, else let them know
The ills we do, their ills instruct us so.

*Emilia* I think it's their husbands' faults if wives stray.
If husbands don't stay faithful and pour their semen that
rightly belongs to us into other women then we need to
point out to them that their wives have sex drives just
like they do.

They fancy other men, they get turned on by the
smell of sex, and like to taste both sweet and sour, just as
husbands do. And don't we have sexual appetites, desires
for having sex? And don't we have a weakness for
succumbing to the temptation of having sex with others,
as men have? Then let them treat us with respect, or
make them understand that when we're unfaithful,
it's only because their sexual misdemeanors teach
us to be so.

Fall. To stray, to be unfaithful.

Treasures. Semen that by right belongs to men's wives. {'Treasure' also means sexual charms, male and female genitals, and women's breasts}

Foreign laps. The vaginas of other women, strangers.

Sense. Sexual desires.

See. To fancy.

Smell. To get turned on.

Affections. Sexual appetites, desires.

Sport. Sexual play.

Frailty. Weakness, succumbing to temptation.

Ills. Their faults, i.e. in being unfaithful

The idea that all women in Shakespeare's time were confined to the home, as domestic drudges subservient to their husbands, and treated merely as creatures to be exchanged in marriage as commercial commodities, has been challenged by recent historians of the period.

Astonishingly, a good proportion of the labour force was made up of women. They worked in almost all the trade guilds as full members, had the equivalent of trade union rights, and worked at the silk trade, as masons, carpenters, farriers, printers, goldsmiths, bootmakers and even as blacksmiths. And perhaps most staggering of all, a recent study of voting registers of the time shows that in some parts of England women regularly voted in parliamentary elections.

# DYING TO COME
## ANTONY AND CLEOPATRA
### *Act 5, Scene 2*

Shakespeare's Cleopatra seems to be in a state of constant
sexual arousal. And whenever her lover Antony is with her,
he is too.

Here, in the company of her serving-maids, the Egyptian Queen
prepares for her death, which she imagines as a sexual union with
the dead Antony.

>*Cleopatra*  Give me my robe. Put on my crown. I have
>
>Immortal longings in me ...
>
>Yare, yare, good Iras, quick – methinks I hear
>
>Antony call. I see him rouse himself
>
>To praise my noble act ...
>
>... Husband, I come.

*Cleopatra* Give me my robe, put on my crown. My cunt must be ready. I have longings to be in heaven {with Antony}. I'm aroused and ready for him. Good Iras, quick – I think I can hear Antony call. I see him sexually excite himself to praise my noble sex-act. Husband, I'm about to come.

Robe. Cunt. {From 'gown'; see page 56}

Crown. Vagina. {A 'crown' is circular. Rings and round objects are puns on vagina, and also on the anus}

Yare. Sexually aroused. {'Yare' is an archaic word meaning eager, brisk and ready, and was a sailing term for a vessel that responds swiftly to the helm and is easily handled. It was used as a punning term for someone who's sexually well-equipped and ready for sex}

Rouse. To excite sexually.

Come. To reach orgasm.

*Pertaining to*

# WANKING

# A FIRM HANDSHAKE

## OTHELLO

### *Act 5, Scene 1*

Iago, the villain who destroys Othello by making him believe his wife Desdemona is a whore, gets the award for the filthiest-minded character in Shakespeare. He has the longest part in the play and almost every one of his 1,070 lines contains a sexual pun. His attitude towards sex is pornographic.

Iago has tricked Othello into believing his wife is having an affair with Cassio, a young lieutenant whom Othello has promoted over Iago. Roderigo, a gullible young man, has been lusting after Desdemona throughout the play, and Iago has promised to help him get her. Here, Iago sets up Roderigo to kill Cassio, using puns on rapier and masturbation to arouse his lust for Desdemona. Iago's language in this dialogue reflects the sexual obsessions and frustrations that underlie his actions throughout the play.

✝

*Iago* Here, stand behind this bulk. Straight will he come.

Wear thy good rapier bare, and put it home.

Quick, quick, fear nothing. I'll be at thy elbow ...

And fix most firm thy resolution.

*Roderigo* Be near at hand. I may miscarry in't.

*Iago* Here at thy hand. Be bold, and take thy stand ...

{*aside*} I have rubbed this young quat almost

   to the sense,

And he grows angry.

✝

*Iago* Here, stand with your erect prick behind this shop, he'll come straight away. Wear your fornicating cock bare, and put it in. Quick, get aroused, don't be afraid of the vagina. I'll be at your knob. Think on that, and fix most firmly on your balls.

*Roderigo* Be near my cock. I might ejaculate too soon.

*Iago* Get your hand going. Be bold, get your prick erect. {*aside*} I've wanked this young pimply little prick almost to climax, and he swells stiff.

Stand. Puns on the idea of the prick 'standing' erect.

Bulk. Shop.

Good. Fornicating.

Rapier. Cock.

Quick. Sexually aroused.

Nothing. Vagina. {There is 'no thing' between a woman's legs, because she lacks a penis. The title of Shakespeare's play *Much Ado About Nothing* means 'Much Ado About Fucking'}

Resolution. Balls. {Relating to liquid (semen) being ejected from swellings (testicles), also to fornication, and to being resolved to act}

Miscarry. To ejaculate prematurely.

Here, at thy hand. Get your hand going, i.e. masturbate.

Rub. To wank.

Quat. Pimple, insignificant person.

Sense. Orgasm.

Grow angry. Become erect.

# A QUIVERING THIGH

## ROMEO AND JULIET

*Act 2, Scene 1*

From the evidence here Romeo's friend Mercutio seems to be obsessed with women's vaginas. In this scene he mocks Romeo for his infatuation with Rosaline, the object of his attentions before he set eyes on Juliet.

Romeo has climbed over a wall into the garden of Juliet's parents' house, and Mercutio calls out to him from the other side of the wall, commanding him to 'appear in the likeness of a sigh'. When Romeo doesn't appear, Mercutio says he'll have to turn conjuror and summon him into his presence by cataloguing Rosaline's sexual attractions.

*Mercutio*  I conjure thee by Rosaline's bright eyes,

By her high forehead and her scarlet lip,

By her fine foot, straight leg, and quivering thigh,

And the demesnes that there adjacent lie . . .

**Mercutio** I *cunt*-jure you by Rosaline's bright cunt, by her high hymen, and her scarlet clitoris, by her admirable rump, straight leg and wanking thigh, and the cunt and arse that there adjacent lie.

Conjure. 'Con-' puns on 'cunt'.
Eyes. Cunt. {The visual allusion is to circles or 'O's}
Scarlet. A colour that symbolises whores. {Also a frequent pun on the scarlet robes of licentious and hypocritical cardinals. Cardinal

Wolsey is called 'scarlet sin' in Shakespeare's *Henry VIII*}
Lip. Clitoris.
Fine foot. A nice or shapely arse.
Quivering. Wanking.
Demesnes. Domains near the thigh, i.e. the cunt and arse.

A rather less sophisticated purveyor of filth was John Wilmot, 2nd Earl of Rochester, who lived more than fifty years after Shakespeare. A notorious libertine, he was played by Johnny Depp in the 2005 film about his life.

Rochester rarely bothered to disguise obscenities with puns, and was certainly never one to describe a woman's genitalia euphemistically. Here, in 'The Imperfect Enjoyment' (c. 1680), the speaker of the poem is talking to his penis, chastising it for not performing:

> 'Worst part of me, and henceforth hated most,
> Through all the town a common fucking-post.
> On whom each whore relieves her tingling cunt
> As hogs on goats do rub themselves and grunt.'

# THE SELFISH GENE

## Sonnet 4

Stop jerking yourself off and ejaculate your spunk in a woman! So says the speaker in the first sonnets of Shakespeare's sequence.

He urges the Young Man to stop masturbating and actually fuck a woman so he can produce a perfect image of his beautiful self.

✝

Unthrifty loveliness, why dost thou spend
Upon thyself thy beauty's legacy? ...
For having traffic with thyself alone,
Thou of thyself thy sweet self dost deceive.

✝

Why do you ejaculate your spunk on yourself when you should use the beauty that Nature gave you to have sex with a woman and reproduce that beauty? Having sex with yourself alone, your wanking yourself off means that you're tricking yourself out of possessing the most intimate part of you – the semen that will create another you.

Spend. To ejaculate.

Beauty's legacy. The beauty given by Nature and the power to create beautiful children.

Traffic with thyself alone. Wanking yourself off.

Sweet. A reference to the genitals, and by extension to semen.

Shakespeare overturned two hundred years of sonnet-writing convention in which the Poet always praises a female Beloved, but never gets beyond the stage of begging her to return his love. There was rarely any question of the love being reciprocated and certainly not of it being consummated. Shakespeare's sonnets are radically different because they show an obsession with the sex-act itself and – even more revolutionary – with the feelings that come after it. And unlike almost all sonnets by other poets, most of his are addressed not to a woman, but to a young man.

# ONE LAST WANK BEFORE I DIE

## HENRY V

### Act 2, Scene 3

Fat John Falstaff died as he had so often done in life - having sex. Shakespeare's original audiences must have been greatly disappointed when they flocked to the first performance of *Henry V*. The epilogue of *Henry IV, Part Two*, the previous play in the series, had suggested that Falstaff would re-appear, but only this description of his death is given.

Here, Mistress 'Quick-Fuck' - brothel keeper and Falstaff's whore - re-enacts the old soldier's last moments. Fittingly, the entire description centres on a death-bed wanking session.

The audience may be in tears, lamenting the loss of a hugely entertaining character, but they are at least consoled with the thought that the old lecher went out with a bang, not a whimper.

*Mistress Quickly*  A made a finer end ... A parted ev'n just between twelve and one, ev'n at the turning o'th'tide - for after I saw him fumble with the sheets, and play with flowers, and smile upon his finger's end, I knew there was but one way. For his nose was as sharp as a pen, and a babbled of green fields. 'How now, Sir John?'

quoth I. 'What, man! Be o'good cheer.' So a cried out, 'God, God, God', three or four times. Now I, to comfort him, bid him a should not think of God . . . So a bade me lay more clothes on his feet. I put my hand into the bed and felt them, and they were as cold as any stone. Then I felt to his knees, and so up'ard and up'ard, and all was as cold as any stone.

*Mistress Quickly* He made a fine end to his life, dying on an orgasm. He departed this life just when he'd got an erection, just at the point when his prick started to go limp.

Because after, when I saw him fumble with himself between the sheets, and toy with his cock, and finger-fuck, I knew there was but one way. His prick was as sharp as a pointed penis, and he played with his penis, and babbled about vaginas.

'What's the matter Sir John?' I said. 'Come along, man! Cheer up!' And he cried out, 'God, God, God', three or four times. So to comfort him, I caressed his prick, and told him he shouldn't worry about God.

So he asked me to lay more clothes on his feet. I put my hand into the bed and felt them, and they were as cold as any testicle. Then I felt to his knees, and so upward and upward, and his prick and arse were as cold as any testicle.

Finer end. 'Fine' means 'consummation', 'end' is 'completed sex'; both words suggest orgasm.

Between twelve and one. With his erection pointing towards twelve as in a dial, and just about to go down. {The image is of the male lying down with his penis pointing up. 'Eleven', from 'leaven', a raising agent, was a pun on the rising of the aroused penis}

Turning of the tide. The penis as it turns from erection towards rest.

Fumble. To play with oneself.

Play with flowers. To toy with one's cock.

Smile upon his finger's end. To finger-fuck.

Nose. Prick.

Pen. Penis.

Babble. A dictionary of the time lists 'the bable of a man' as meaning penis. {The suggestion here is of 'talking out of his cock'}

Green fields. Female genitals. {As in a women's 'fields' sown by male seed}

Stone. Testicle.

Falstaff spends his life – and his semen – in the brothel. He's an expert at sexual puns, and the provoker of some of Mistress Quickly's best unintended double entendres. His is a dream of a part for actors. One particular Falstaffian gem comes in *Henry IV Part One*, 3.3, where Sir John asks for a bawdy song to make him horny. He then remarks that:

> *'I was as virtuously given as a gentleman need to be; virtuous enough; swore little; diced not – above seven times a week; went to a bawdy-house – once in a quarter – of an hour.'*

# A BOBBING PUCK

## A MIDSUMMER NIGHT'S DREAM

### *Act 2, Scene 1*

Puck, jester to Oberon and Titania, the King and Queen of the Fairies, is a fine dealer in filth.

He thinks human beings and their silly love games are a joke: 'Lord, what fools these mortals be!' He takes a fiendish delight in their squabbles, their pain and their distress. Here, Puck turns to the audience and tells us the following surreally dirty tale.

> *Puck* I am that merry wanderer of the night.
>
> I jest to Oberon, and make him smile . . .
>
> And sometime lurk I in a gossip's bowl
>
> In very likeness of a roasted crab,
>
> And when she drinks, against her lips I bob,
>
> And on her withered dewlap pour the ale.

*Puck* I am that horny wanderer of the night. I tell fart jokes to Oberon, and make him smell them. And sometimes I lurk in an old whore's pelvis in the perfect disguise of a roasted crab. And when she drinks, I wank against her cunt, and ejaculate my spunk on her shrivelled-up cunt lips.

Merry. Horny.

Jest. To fart.

Smile. To smell.

Gossip. Old whore.

Bowl. Pelvis.

Lips. Cunt lips.

Bob. To wank.

Dewlap. Vaginal folds, cunt.

Ale. Spunk. {The image is of froth floating on the ale}

In a compendious volume of words, the lexicographer Randale Cotgrave meticulously recorded the language of French and English. *A Dictionarie of the French and English Tongues* was printed in London in 1611. It is thanks to Cotgrave that we can find out many of the meanings of sexual puns in Shakespeare's time. Here's how Cotgrave listed the word 'dewlap':

> '*The deaw-lap in a womans Privities. Whence defchiquetée. An ouglie nickname for an overridden Hackney (or Harlot).*'

# *Pertaining to*
# CUNNILINGUS

# TIPPING THE VELVET

## CYMBELINE

### Act 2, Scene 3

Cloten is one of Shakespeare's would-be rapists, and one of his most odious characters. His name is pronounced like clot-pole - he's a thick clot with little brain. He's the son of the Queen by her previous marriage. She is now married to the King of Britain, Cymbeline.

With his wicked mother's connivance, Cloten plots to marry Innogen, the daughter of Cymbeline. First, he wants to rape her ...

*Cloten* If I could get this foolish Innogen I should have gold enough. It's almost morning, is't not?

*First Lord* Day, my lord.

*Cloten* I would this music would come. I am advised to give her music o' mornings; they say it will penetrate.

　　　{Enter *Musicians*}

Come on, tune. If you can penetrate her with your fingering, so; we'll try with tongue too. If none will do, let her remain; but I'll never give o'er.

*Cloten* If I could fuck this whorish Innogen I should have gold enough. It's almost morning isn't it?

*First Lord* Day, my lord.

*Cloten* I wish this music would come. I've been advised to give her music in the mornings; they say it will get her sexually aroused.

{*Enter Musicians*}

Come on, get your tools ready. If you can finger-fuck her, OK. I'll try oral sex as well. If nothing succeeds in fucking her and getting her to respond, let her remain; but I'll never give up.

Get. i.e. fuck.
Foolish. Whorish, wanton.
Penetrate. i.e. as the music penetrates her ear, he'll be able to penetrate her vagina. {The suggestion is that he needs the music to seduce her, because he certainly won't be able to seduce her without it}
Tune. Get your tool ready.
Penetrate with fingering. Finger-fuck.
Try with tongue. Try oral sex, try cunnilingus.

There is another rape plot in the play. The Roman Jachimo has a wager with Innogen's husband, Leonatus, that Jachimo can get his wife to sleep with him. As Jachimo creeps towards Innogen's bedchamber he compares himself to one of the most famous rapists in ancient history – Tarquin, the Roman tyrant who raped Lucretia (a story told in Shakespeare's narrative poem *The Rape of Lucrece*, see page 245). And there is an allusion to yet another rape: the book Innogen had been reading when she fell asleep is the story – told in Ovid – of Tereus who raped Philomela and cut out her tongue. The story is also referred to in Shakespeare's *Titus Andronicus*.

# GRAZING RIGHTS
## VENUS AND ADONIS

*Lines 229–234*

Readers in Shakespeare's day clearly loved their poetry sexy. And his long poem *Venus and Adonis* did not disappoint them: startlingly erotic, often bristling with sexual heat, and, in the end, unbearably tragic, it took erotic poetry to giddy new heights. *Venus and Adonis* was a monster hit.

Shakespeare's goddess in *Venus and Adonis* is fleshy, rank, her body sweats and 'her face doth reek and smoke'. Such is the extent of her lust for the young boy Adonis that she is in a constant state of arousal. She does everything to seduce him, but Shakespeare has made his Adonis an unripened, seemingly sexless mortal, coldly chaste and completely immune to the goddess's charms.

> 'Fondling,' she saith, 'since I have hemmed thee here
>
> Within the circuit of this ivory pale,
>
> I'll be a park, and thou shalt be my deer.
>
> Feed where thou wilt, on mountain or in dale;
>
>  Graze on my lips, and if those hills be dry,
>
>  Stray lower, where the pleasant fountains lie.'

'My sweet foolish beloved,' she said, 'since I've hemmed you here inside my embracing arms, pretend my body's a park and you can be my deer.

'Taste wherever you want, on my breasts and rump, or in the valley of my vagina. Graze on my lips, and if those hills be dry, stray lower to those other lips, where my pleasure-giving sexual juices lie.'

| | |
|---|---|
| Circuit of this ivory pale. Her embracing white arms. | Dale. An open valley, i.e. the vagina. |
| Park. A word often used to refer to the topography of the female body. | Lips. Outer folds surrounding the vagina. |
| Deer. Punning on 'dear'. | Pleasant. Pleasure-giving. |
| Mountain. Breasts. | Fountains. Sexual emissions. |

Every stanza of this poem is erotically charged – it's as if an electric current is rippling through it. Shakespeare dedicated the poem to the 19-year-old Earl of Southampton. It was the first of his works to appear in print, and was an instant best-seller – it went through no fewer than nine editions, and was often printed in poetry anthologies, and frequently quoted by other writers at the time.

All the copies of the handsomely produced volume were read and re-read until they fell to pieces – it seems there is only one copy still in existence. In a series of plays performed by Cambridge undergraduates a few years later, a 'Sweet Mr Shakespeare' is referred to, and to honour him, a character named Gullio says he will 'lay his Venus and Adonis under my pillow'.

# FRENCH LEAVE

## HENRY V

### *Act 2, Scene 3*

Pistol, a coward and a bully, married to the brothel madam, Mistress Quickly, roars through Shakespeare's history plays like a sex dictionary on legs. He's off to the war in France and wants to make sure his wife keeps their brothel open and their whores busy.

He's particularly anxious that his wife won't let the punters get serviced on credit. He's worried, too, that the prostitutes might get lazy and not keep up their pleasuring techniques.

*Pistol {To Mistress Quickly}* ... My love, give me thy lips.

{*He kisses her*}

Look to my chattels and my movables.

Let senses rule. The word is 'Pitch and pay' ...

{*To his friends*}

- Yokefellows in arms,

Let us to France, like horseleeches, my boys,

To suck, to suck, the very blood to suck! . . .

{*To Mistress Quickly*}

Let housewifery appear. Keep close, I thee command.

*Pistol* {*To Mistress Quickly*} My love, give me your lips.
{*He kisses her*} Look after my whores, and get them to
use all their every sexual skill to gratify the customers'
lust. And don't forget the prostitute's motto: it's cash
down, no credit, if they want to thrust in and get their
end away.

{*To his friends*}

Fellows joined together in arms, let's go to France, like
licking whores, my boys, to suck, to suck, the very
spunk to suck!

{*To Mistress Quickly*}

Bawd, I order you to keep a close eye on the whores of
our tavern, and make sure they keep up their lusty
ways.

Lips. Cunt.

Chattels. Whores.

Movables. Whores.

Senses. As a verb, 'sense' means 'to gratify lust'.

Pitch. To thrust in, to whore. {A 'pitch' is also a venereally infectious whore}

Pay. To have sex.

Horse. Whore.

Leeches. The worms were believed to be a cure for venereal diseases, and the word also carries a suggestion of sexual 'licking'.

Blood. Spunk.

Housewifery. Whoring.

Appear. To have sex.

Keep. As a noun 'keep' meant a bawd or prostitute.

Close. Lusty.

*Pertaining to*

# FELLATIO

# A GOOD FROTH

## THE TWO GENTLEMEN
## OF VERONA

### *Act 3, Scene 1*

This ribald exchange of sexual puns is centred on a very desirable attribute in a female lover. Lance, the servant of one of the play's heroes, Proteus, has been reading out from a list he's made of the virtues and vices of his beloved. Speed, the servant of the other hero, Valentine, arrives, grabs the list and reads from it.

What adds to the comedy of the scene is that every item on the list repeatedly puns on the same sexual skill. Each one refers to the ability of Lance's girlfriend to give sexual pleasure in general, and to 'milk' the penis – in more ways than one – in particular.

*Lance* I am in love . . . 'tis a milkmaid . . . '*Imprimis*, she can fetch and carry . . . *Item*, she can milk.' Look you, a sweet virtue in a maid with clean hands.

{*Enter Speed. He takes the list*}

*Speed* '*Imprimis*, she can milk.'

*Lance* Ay, that she can.

*Speed* '*Item*, she brews good ale . . . *Item*, she can sew . . . *Item*, she hath a sweet mouth.'

**Lance**  That makes amends for her sour breath.

**Speed**  ... 'Item, she hath no teeth ...'

**Lance**  Well, the best is, she hath no teeth to bite.

**Lance**  I am in love. She's a woman who can masturbate me.

In the first place, she can wank me off and bear the weight of me.

Also, she can jerk me off. Now that's a sweet virtue in a young woman with clean hands.

　　　{*Enter Speed. He takes the list*}

**Speed**  In the first place, she can wank you off.

**Lance**  Too right, that she can.

**Speed**  Also, she brings forth a good spunk froth. Also, she can make spunk ooze out. Also, she has a mouth that can make you come.

**Lance**  That makes amends for her sour breath.

**Speed**  Also, she has no teeth.

**Lance**  Well, the best thing about that is, she's got no teeth to bite me when she's giving me a blow job.

Milkmaid. A woman who 'milks' (masturbates) the penis.

Imprimis. In the first place, a Latin phrase used to begin a list.

Fetch. To draw forth semen, to masturbate.

Carry. To bear the weight of a lover.

Milk. To masturbate. {As a noun, 'milk' also meant semen}

Brew good ale. To produce a large amount of semen. {The allusion is to the head or froth that accumulates in the brewing of ale}

Sew. To make semen ooze out. {Punning on the 'sowing' or scattering of seeds}

Sweet. Make sweetness, i.e. masturbate. {The French word *suites* denoted the balls of a wild boar}

No teeth to bite. No teeth to bite his penis during fellatio. {'To bite' meant to fuck, and to castrate, and is here perhaps a pun from the French *potage de la bite* (literally, 'soup of the cock'), which means 'semen'}

# MISTRESS QUICK-FUCK SAYS 'NO' TO A DRINK

## HENRY IV, PART TWO,

### *Act 2, Scene 4*

Whenever she opens her mouth Mistress Quickly utters a sexual pun without knowing it. And she never recognises a sexual undertone when it's brought to the surface and obvious to all. On the other hand, she has a unique ability to pronounce and interpret harmless words as vulgar puns. She is, in keeping with her profession, a butt of men's jokes in the tavern.

When Shakespeare came to write the follow-up to the first part of *Henry IV*, he introduced two new characters into the tavern in Eastcheap. One was the swaggering, bombastic Pistol, whose very name means a penis constantly firing off; the other was the whore Doll Tearsheet, whose name is a wonderfully graphic description of her frenzied athletics in bed.

> *Falstaff* Welcome, Ensign Pistol. Here, Pistol, I charge you with a cup of sack. Do you discharge upon mine hostess.
>
> *Pistol* I will discharge upon her, Sir John, with two bullets.

*Falstaff* She is pistol-proof, sir, you shall not hardly offend her.

*Mistress Quickly* Come, I'll drink no proofs, nor no bullets. I'll drink no more than will do me good, for no man's pleasure, I.

*Falstaff* Welcome, Ensign Penis. Here, Penis, I toast you with a cup of sack. Now return the toast and ejaculate into my hostess.

*Pistol* I will ejaculate into her, Sir John, with the spunk from my two balls.

*Falstaff* She's penis-proof, sir, you won't be able to test your manhood on her. You'll hardly violate her.

*Mistress Quickly* Get away with you, I'll drink from no balls, I'll drink no spunk. I'll drink no more than will do me good, not for any man's sexual pleasure, not I.

Pistol. Penis.
Charge. To toast. {Also punning on the idea of 'loading' with ammunition}
Discharge. To ejaculate.

Bullets. Balls full of spunk.
Offend. To violate. {Falstaff is saying that Pistol will be unable to penetrate Mistress Quickly's vagina}

Long before Shakespeare's day, London was known for excessive drinking. The historian John Stow recorded that the problem of drunkenness got so bad that 200 alehouses in the city were closed down in 1574. But that still left hundreds of taverns – such as Mistress Quickly's Boar's Head – selling ale and beer from the 58 ale brewers and 33 beer brewers in the city. A young Venetian merchant visiting London complained that the beer tasted disgusting and was cloudy like horse's piss. People generally believed that brewers used foul Thames water in the making of ale.

Shakespeare seems to have had a particular aversion to alcohol's effects on the libido. In *Macbeth* 2.3 the Porter says drink 'provokes desire, but it takes away the performance ... it makes him stand to, and not stand to [causes an erection and then makes it droop]'.

Tobacco seems to have affected Londoners' sex lives as well. Women do not appear to have smoked – not in public, anyway, although women who dressed up as men did. One wife complained to her husband that 'It makes your breath stink like the piss of a fox.' London was clearly a city of heavy smokers. According to Barnaby Riche's play *The Honesty of this Age* (1614), there was one tobacco shop for every Londoner, and visitors from abroad commented on men

*'lighting up on all occasions ... and it makes them riotous ... as if they were drunk ... I am told the inside of one man's veins after death was found to be covered in soot just like a chimney ...'*

# *Pertaining to*
# BUGGERY

# INDECENT EXPOSURE

## ROMEO AND JULIET

### *Act 2, Scene 1*

Perhaps the dirtiest lines in Shakespeare are delivered by Romeo's friend Mercutio, one of the most foul-mouthed of his characters. But audiences tend to forgive him anything because when he comes on stage he lights it up. And because his sexual bantering is not only outrageous, it's also witty.

A line in this extract where Mercutio is imagining Romeo dreaming of sex with his first love Rosaline, was censored in Shakespeare's own lifetime. One edition replaced the phrase 'open-arse' with 'open *Et Caetera*', and a later one left a blank: 'open, or—'

*Mercutio* If love be blind, love cannot hit the mark.

Now will he sit under a medlar tree

And wish his mistress were that kind of fruit

As maids call medlars when they laugh alone.

O Romeo, that she were, O that she were

An open-arse, and thou a popp'rin' pear.

*Mercutio*  If love be blind, he won't be able to fuck the vagina. He'll sit under a medlar tree and wish his mistress were that kind of fruit that girls call open-arses when they're talking dirty on their own. O Romeo, if only she were, O if only she were an open arse, and you an erect penis popping it in her.

Hit. To fuck. {A pun from archery}
Mark. Vagina. {The archery terms 'mark' and 'target' were frequent puns on female genitals}
Medlar. Fruit of the medlar tree that is only edible when over-ripe. {'Open-arse' was a slang term for a medlar, the shape of the fruit being thought to resemble the anus. In *Timon of Athens*, 4.3, Timon says he hates the medlar because it looks like the churlish philosopher Apemantus, i.e. it looks like his open arse}
Laugh. A word that often suggests bawdry. It was a pun on making love, causing an erection, and farting. Given Mercutio's coarse mind, he's probably imagining the girls are laughing at obscene matters.
Popp'rin' pear. Erect penis, punning on 'pop her in'. {A pear from the Flemish town of *Poperinghe* (now in Belgium) that was shaped like an erect penis}

*Romeo and Juliet* is one of the most famous tragedies about love in Western literature. It is also one of Shakespeare's bawdiest plays. Its plethora of sexual puns gives the play a levity which some critics have found inappropriate. What is remarkable, though, is the way that these puns – which are an essentially comic device – serve the tragic development of the play. It is often said that with *Romeo and Juliet*, Shakespeare tricked his audience with an opening that signalled the possibilities of comedy only to discard them and turn the play into a tragedy.

# COMING. . .
# UP THE REAR
## HENRY IV, PART TWO
### *Act 3, Scene 2*

Shakespeare's towering comic character Falstaff is a liar,
a thief, a glutton, a drunkard and a sponger – and audiences
can never get enough of him.

Here, he reminisces about his old friend, Justice Shallow, and the
wild days of their youth.

*Falstaff* I do see the bottom of Justice Shallow. Lord,

Lord, how subject we old men are to this vice of lying!

This same starved justice hath done nothing but prate to

me of the wildness of his youth ... When a was naked,

he was for all the world like a forked radish, with a head

fantastically carved upon it with a knife ... A came ever

in the rearward of the fashion ...

✝

*Falstaff* I can see the bottom of Justice Shallow. Lord, Lord, how subject we old men are to this vice of fucking! This homosexual deformed whore has done nothing but talk out of his arse to me about the wildness of his youth. When he was naked, his rump looked for all the world like a forked radish, with a foreskin fantastically carved upon it as if with a knife. He reached orgasm always in the sodomite's style – in the division of the buttocks.

Justice. Whore.

Lying. Fucking.

Same. Homosexual. {The Greek *homos* means 'same'}

Starved. Deformed, disabled, paralysed.

Prate. To talk out of one's arse. {From 'prat', meaning arse, buttocks}

Forked. 'Fork' refers to the buttocks and upper thigh.

Head. Foreskin.

Came. Reached orgasm, ejaculated.

In the rearward of the fashion. Fucked like a sodomite, i.e. from behind, in the division of the buttocks, in the arse.

In Shakespeare's day the legal definition of sodomy or buggery was a narrow one. For a prosecution, the act had to be rape, i.e. forced on somebody against their will. It had to involve penetration and ejaculation, *and there had to be a witness.* Sodomy was a capital offence – those convicted were put to death by hanging. But there were very few convictions for sodomy in Shakespeare's time. In the Home County Assizes, for example, only one man was convicted for sodomy over a period of 68 years.

The only cases of sodomy that the law of the time appears to have taken seriously were those involving the rape of boys under the age of consent. Before 1607 the age of consent was 14, but after that date it was raised to 21.

The whole question of society's view of homosexual acts in Shakespeare's time was a complicated one. The practice was publicly condemned as an abomination, but in practice there seems to have been a tacit acceptance of it. As long as it did not involve violence or disrupt the social order, the authorities generally chose to ignore it. The British Parliament finally decriminalised homosexual acts between consenting adults in July 1967.

*Pertaining to*

# TRANSVESTITE

# BOYS WILL
# BE GIRLS WILL
# BE BOYS

## AS YOU LIKE IT

### *Epilogue*

In 16th-century England 'Ganymede' was a byword for
male–male sex, and in particular for the younger, passive male
partner in a homosexual relationship. In Greek mythology,
Jove, king of the gods, fell in love with the boy Ganymede
and took him up to heaven to be his 'cup-bearer', or young
male lover.

By calling the cross-dressed heroine Ganymede, Shakespeare was able to
suggest a homoerotic element to Orlando's feelings for the 'boy'. But the
situation is even more complicated than this. All the women's parts in
the plays of the time were played by boy-actors or 'play-boys'. However
convincing they were as women, there is little doubt that audiences
remained aware that the body beneath the dress was male. And that the
body was sexually provocative to both men and women in the audience.

 This gives the encounters between Orlando and Rosalind/Gany-
mede a kind of double sexual frisson. On one level, it is two males
flirting with one another; on another level, it's a male and
female flirting.

 The play ends with a delicious sexual tease. 'Ganymede' leaves the
stage and comes back without the male disguise, as Rosalind. But then in
the Epilogue Rosalind reminds the audience that 'she' is really a 'he' – the
boy actor playing her part. The confusion of sexual identities reaches its
dizzying climax when, having stripped off his disguises, the male actor

does not bow, but *curtsies* to the playgoers. By the time the speech comes to an end we don't know *who* is speaking to the audience. The figure on stage remains a tantalising male-female.

✝

*Rosalind* It is not the fashion to see the lady in the epilogue ... My way is to conjure you; and I'll begin with the women. I charge you, O women, for the love you bear to men, to like as much of this play as please you. And I charge you, O men, for the love you bear to women ... that between you and the women the play may please. If I were a woman I would kiss as many of you as had beards that pleased me, complexions that liked me, and breaths that I defied not. And I am sure, as many as have good beards, or good faces, or sweet breaths will for my kind offer, when I make curtsy, bid me farewell.

✝

*Rosalind* It's not usual to see the actor playing the play's heroine in the epilogue. What I like to do is to shag you, and I'll begin with the women. I charge you, O women, for the love you give to men when shagging them, to like as much of this play as gives you sexual pleasure. And I charge you, O men, for the love you give to women, that between you and your women the play will give you both sexual pleasure when you get home. If I were a woman I would shag as many of you as had pubes and pricks that gave me sexual pleasure, complexions that turned me on, and gave me shags that I wouldn't want to reject. And I am sure that just as many of you as have good pubes, or good arses, or balls filled with spunk, will, in response to my offer of sexual favours when I curtsy, wish me farewell with your applause.

Conjure. To shag. {Sexual congress, from the French *congrès*, meeting}
Bear. To bear the weight of a sexual partner, i.e. to have sex.
Please. To please sexually.
Kiss. To have sexual intercourse. {A term in billiards for when the balls are shot and brush against one another while in motion}
Beards. Pubic hair.
Breaths. Shags, fucks.

Faces. Arses. {From the French *fesses*, meaning buttocks)
Sweet breaths. Balls filled with spunk. {'Sweets' is a pun on testicles. French *suites* are the balls of a wild boar}
Kind offer. Sexual favours. {'Kind' refers to sex and gender. 'Kindly' is a play on 'kindle', to inflame with sexual desire}
Bid me farewell. i.e with applause.

A notorious female transvestite of the time was Mary Frith, known as Moll Cutpurse and the subject of a play by Thomas Middleton and Thomas Dekker called *The Roaring Girl* (1611).

Born the daughter of a middle-class shoemaker, she adopted male dress, became rich as a thief and forger, and claimed to be the manager of an international chain of brothels. Moll seems to have believed in equality: not only did she provide young women for men, she also procured male lovers for middle-class wives. One young wife who made frequent use of Moll's services had twelve children, but only the first was her husband's. She also got fathers to pay up for their illegitimate children.

The Puritans railed against her; Londoners loved her. She became such a popular celebrity that in 1611 she performed a solo show at the Fortune Theatre, singing and playing the lute and wearing breeches and sword.

# COCKING A SNOOK
## THE TWO GENTLEMEN OF VERONA
### *Act 2, Scene 7*

We know that female prostitutes in Shakespeare's time dressed in men's clothes to make them more erotically desirable to their male clients. Female transvestism was a quite common practice, although it was the subject of hysterical disapproval by the moral police force because the women who wore masculine attire were demonstrating a dangerous independence.

It was not that they wanted to be like men, but because they saw cross-dressing as empowering, a bid for freedom from the rules laid down for them by men. It was a way of putting up two fingers to the establishment, and saying 'I have the sexual freedom to do what I like.'

Shakespeare's heroines dressed as boys provoked men's desire as well as women's in the audience because they were simultaneously heterosexual and homosexual. This ambiguity was seen as erotically alluring to both sexes.

Here, Julia, one of the heroines of *The Two Gentlemen of Verona*, is discussing with her waiting-woman, Lucetta, what clothes she needs to have made in order to dress up as a boy. The most important item of clothing, she is told, is the codpiece, which was so heavily stuffed with padding to make it stick up and out that it made men look as though they walked about with permanent erections.

Julia, worried that her disguise will bring disgrace on her, is drawing attention to the puritanical outrage against women who dared to disrupt the difference between the sexes.

*Lucetta* What fashion, madam, shall I make your breeches? ... You must needs have them with a codpiece, madam.

*Julia* Out, out, Lucetta. That will be ill-favoured.

*Lucetta* A round hose, madam, now's not worth a pin Unless you have a codpiece to stick pins on ...

*Julia* ... how will the world repute me For undertaking so unstaid a journey? I fear me it will make me scandalized.

*Lucetta* How do you want your false penis to look, madam, in your trousers? You've got to have them with a codpiece, madam.

*Julia* Oh no, no, Lucetta. That will make me look awful.

*Lucetta* A round penis, madam, is now not worth calling a penis unless you have a codpiece covering that pricks can fuck on.

*Julia* How will the world judge me for undertaking such an unladylike journey? I'm scared I'll cause a scandal.

Fashion. Penis. {Punning on the Latin *fascinum*, penis}
Codpiece. A pouch covering the male genitals. {See page 99}.
Hose. Penis.
Pin. Prick. {Codpieces were thickly padded and could be used as pin-cushions for keeping ruff pins handy. Ruffs were pinned on to the neckline of a dress or jacket with hundreds of pins, and often some of the pins would shoot out from the ruff if the wearer made a sudden movement}
Stick. Fornicate. {The French *foutre* means 'to stick', or 'to fuck]
Unstaid. Unladylike, unbecoming, unseemly (in a woman).

An anonymous pamphlet of the time denounced women who dressed as men and called them harlots. The author describes one woman's costume as having 'the loose, lascivious civil embracement of a French doublet, being all unbuttoned to entice (revealing naked breasts) ... and extreme short waisted to give most easy way to every luxurious [lascivious] action ... most ruffianly [whorish] short hair' and a sword *(Hic Mulier or The Man-Woman).*

This shows that the female transvestite was hardly trying to look like a man. What it does show is that the costume was worn to display female charms and at the same time flaunt the wearer's sexual freedom. Women who also wore a codpiece would have offered the particularly striking image of a double-sexed being.

# *Pertaining to*
# LESBIAN

# GENDER-BENDING

## TWELFTH NIGHT

### Act 1, Scene 5

How stable is our sexual identity? Shakespeare showed his fascination with this question in a number of his plays. Seven of his women characters dress up as males, and the confusion and ambiguities that emerge from their sexual disguise invite the audience to question their assumptions about the subject.

Shipwrecked in Illyria, Viola is parted from her identical twin brother, Sebastian, whom she believes has drowned. To survive, she dresses up as a boy, calls herself Cesario, and gets work as the page of Duke Orsino who is in love with a beautiful heiress, the countess Olivia.
When Orsino sends Viola/Cesario to Olivia with his avowals of love, the heiress falls instantly in love with the 'boy'. Shakespeare makes clear that Viola/Cesario's disguise is not completely convincing: the Duke describes Cesario's appearance as decidedly feminine, with lips smooth and ruby-like and a voice like a maiden's.

That Olivia is instantly attracted to a young man who looks like a young woman carries a coded suggestion of lesbianism. When Cesario leaves after their first meeting, Olivia is seized with a fierce passion. She says that she 'feels this youth's perfections'; 'perfection' meaning having both male and female elements.

*Olivia* Thy tongue, thy face, thy limbs, actions, and
  spirit
Do give thee five-fold blazon. Not too fast. Soft, soft –
... How now?
Even so quickly may one catch the plague?
Methinks I feel this youth's perfections
With an invisible and subtle stealth
To creep in at mine eyes. Well, let it be.

*Olivia* Your genitals, your arse, your limbs, your
sexually provocative actions, and your spunk loudly
proclaim you to all the world. Not too fast: stop! stop!
How has this happened? Is this how you can get so
quickly aroused, as fast as catching the plague? I think I
must be attracted to this perfect girl-boy. Feel her-him
creep in at my vagina with an invisible and subtle
stealth. Well, let it happen.

Tongue. Clitoris, penis.

Face. Arse. {Punning on the French *fesses*, buttocks}

Actions. Sexually provocative actions.

Spirit. Spunk.

Five-fold blazon. To proclaim something loudly and publicly. {'Blazon' is a term in heraldry that denotes a gentleman's coat of arms. It can also mean something colourful and ostentatious}

Quickly. The suggestion here is of the speed of sexual arousal.

Perfection. Hermaphrodite, a being combining male and female attributes.

Eyes. Orifices, punning on vagina. {The visual allusion is to circles or 'O's'; 'eyes' also denote the anus and testicles}

Sappho, who lived some time around the 6th century BC, is often called the patron saint of lesbians. All we know about her life is that she lived on the island of Lesbos, in the Aegean Sea, and that readers of the time thought her the greatest of lyric poets and admired her. John Donne, a contemporary of Shakespeare, wrote a poem, 'Sapho (*sic*) to Philaenis', in which Sappho praises her female lover:

> 'Thy body is a natural Paradise,
> In whose self, unmanur'd all pleasure lies,
> Nor needs Perfection; why shouldst thou then
> Admit the tillage of a harsh, rough man?'

# MISTRESS PAGE: 'IS HER VAGINA AT HOME? I'M LONGING TO SEE HER'

## THE MERRY WIVES OF WINDSOR

### Act 3, Scene 2

The fiercely possessive Ford is in constant fear of his wife being unfaithful. And not just with a man. He implies that his wife and her friend Mistress Page have a lesbian relationship.

Here, Mistress Page rejects the insinuation, but Shakespeare gives her plenty of puns rich in suggestive undertones of same-sex desire.

**Ford** Well met, Mistress Page. Whither go you?

**Mistress Page** Truly, sir, to see your wife. Is she at home?

**Ford** Ay, and as idle as she may hang together, for want of company. I think if your husbands were dead you two would marry.

**Mistress Page** Be sure of that – two other husbands . . .

Is your wife at home indeed?

*Ford*  Indeed she is.

*Mistress Page*  . . . I am sick till I see her.

*Ford*  Well met, whore flesh, Mistress Page. Where are you going to have sex?

*Mistress Page*  I'll tell you, to see your wife. Is her vagina at home?

*Ford*  Yes, and she's so lusty I think she'll whore herself for hire. I reckon if your husbands were dead you two would marry.

*Mistress Page*  Be sure of that – two other husbands. . . . Is your wife at home having an orgasm?

*Ford*  Yes, she's having sex.

*Mistress Page*  I'm full of sexual longing till I see her.

| | |
|---|---|
| Well. Whore. {Punning on a 'well', which receives liquid} | Idle. Lusty. |
| Met. Punning on 'meat', i.e. flesh. | Hang together. To whore oneself for hire, to pander. |
| Go. To have sex. | Indeed. Having an orgasm, having |
| Home. Vagina. | sex. {'To do' is 'to fuck'} |

Plays of the time frequently used 'well' as a pun on vagina. One of the funniest is by Shakespeare's fellow playwright, John Marston. In *The Dutch Courtesan* (1605), a witty rogue called Cocledemoy (probably meaning 'Cuckold Me') lists the attributes of bawds, concluding that they 'both live well and die well, since most commonly they live in Clerkenwell, and die in Bridewell' (2.1). Clerkenwell was one of London's brothel districts and Bridewell was a 'house of correction' where whores and vagrants were sent and made to do an honest day's work.

# THE DOUBLE CHERRY

## A MIDSUMMER NIGHT'S DREAM

### Act 3, Scene 2

Helena's passion for her childhood friend Hermia makes for one of the most realistic, heartfelt speeches of jealousy in the whole of Shakespeare.

When she believes her friend has betrayed her with the two young men of the play, she looks back on the life they shared.

*Helena* Injurious Hermia, most ungrateful maid . . .

Is all the counsel that we two have shared –

The sisters' vows, the hours that we have spent . . .

O, is all quite forgot? . . .

Both warbling of one song . . .

Like to a double cherry: seeming parted,

But yet an union in partition,

Two lovely berries moulded on one stem.

So, with two seeming bodies but one heart . . .

And will you rend our ancient love asunder,

To join with men in scorning your poor friend?

✝

*Helena* Backbiting Hermia, most ungrateful maid, are all the secrets of our cunts that we two have shared, the sisters' vows, the hours that we two have spent. O, have you forgotten all this? Both fucking as one, reaching orgasm, at the same time, like a double vagina: seeming separate but united as one. Two lovely sets of genitals formed on one stem, seeming to have two bodies but one heart. And will you tear apart our ancient love, to have sex with men and scorn your lesbian friend?

Counsel. Secrets of their bodies. {'Coun-' plays on 'cunt'} Warbling of one song. Fucking as one. {'Sing' and 'song' are puns on fucking} Double. Same-sex love. Double cherry. The reference is to two sets of female genitals. Berries. Genitals. Join. To have sex with. Poor. Lesbian. {Punning on 'pure', meaning same-sex love; it is 'pure' because only one sex is involved}

The ancient Greek philosopher Plato called lesbians 'female companions'. He said originally a woman had two sets of everything, including genitals. The god Jove sliced them in half and from these two halves came lesbians who long for other women to love and find completion with.

From the beginning of the 19th century, directors of *A Midsummer Night's Dream* have often felt uncomfortable with Helena's speech and have routinely cut the more erotic of the lines. The actor-manager F.R. Benson (1858–1939) cut the whole speech and even in the 1950s the last three passionate lines were cut.

# INTIMATE KNOWLEDGE

## AS YOU LIKE IT

### Act 1, Scene 3

Women who have erotic feelings for other women appear in several of Shakespeare's plays.

When Rosalind, the heroine of *As You Like It*, is banished from the court by Duke Frederick, her friend Celia's father, Celia doesn't think twice about abandoning her father, her fortune, and her social status at court to join Rosalind in exile in the Forest of Arden. The Duke's courtier suggests the intimacy of their relationship when he says their 'loves are dearer than the natural bond of sisters'.

In erotically charged language, Celia throws a lover's strop, rebuking Rosalind for not loving her as much as she loves her. Here she declares to Duke Frederick that she cannot live without her dear friend.

*Celia*  We still have slept together,

Rose at an instant, learned, played, eat together,

And wheresoe'er we went, like Juno's swans

Still we went coupled and inseparable . . .

I cannot live out of her company.

*Celia* We have always slept together. Got aroused at the same moment, learned our lessons, enjoyed intimacies, had sex together. And wherever we went, we were like the paired swans that drew Juno through the heavens. We always reached orgasm in sexual union at the same time, and were inseparable. I cannot live out of her company.

Rose. Became sexually aroused. Played. Enjoyed sexual intimacies. Eat together. To feed off one another in an erotic sense, i.e. to have sex. {In *Othello*, 3.4, Iago's wife Emilia says that men 'are all but stomachs, and we (women) all but food. / They eat us hungrily, and when they are full / They belch us.'} Juno's swans. Paired swans that drew the chariot of Juno, queen of the gods, through the heavens. Still. Always. Went. Came, i.e. experienced orgasm. Coupled. Paired in sexual intercourse.

Throughout her reign there was endless speculation about Queen Elizabeth I's sexual tastes. Apart from rumours about her heterosexual relations – some claimed that she bore bastard children by her supposed lover Robert Dudley, the Earl of Leicester – there were whisperings that she had sexual relations with women. Elizabeth herself once joked that she should marry a Princess and play the husband's role in the relationship.

*Pertaining to*

# HOMOSEXUAL

# CORIOL-ANUS

## CORIOLANUS

### Act 4, Scene 5

Coriolanus offers an astonishingly potent mix of violence and male homoeroticism. In performance, the exchanges between Coriolanus and Aufidius pack such a powerful punch, they have an almost visceral impact on the audience.

When the two warriors, Coriolanus and Aufidius, meet in one-to-one combat, their wrestling resembles some frenzied sexual clasping of pleasure and pain. In a world dominated by military values, where blood shed in battle is worn as a mark of honour, even enemies can act like lovers – they need one another to reinforce an identity that is defined solely by their prowess on the battlefield. Aufidius's speech here suggests an orgasmic outpouring of emotion for his enemy.

*Aufidius* Let me twine

Mine arms about {thy} body . . .

I loved the maid I married . . .

But that I see thee here,

Thou noble thing, more dances my rapt heart

Than when I first my wedded mistress saw

Bestride my threshold . . . and I have nightly since

Dreamt of encounters 'twixt thyself and me –

We have been down together in my sleep,
Unbuckling helms, fisting each other's throat -
And waked half dead with nothing.

*Aufidius* Let me coil my arms around your body.
I loved the maid I married, but when I see you here, see
your impressive cock, my captivated heart dances more
than when I first saw my wedded mistress astride my
prick. Every night I've dreamt of erotic encounters
between you and me. We've fucked each other in my
sleep, unbuckling each other's helmets, fisting each
other's throats, and woken up half dead from fucking.

Noble thing. Impressive cock.
{'Thing' is a pun on penis, and
also on vagina}
Threshold. Prick. {Punning also
on 'thresh' and 'thrash' in the
sense of 'fuck'}
Been down together. Fucked each
other. {'To down' was also a pun
meaning 'to whore'}
Nothing. Fucking. {As well as
punning on female genitals (there
is 'nothing', i.e. no penis, between a
woman's legs), 'nothing' often puns
on musical 'noting' or 'pricking' of
notes. 'Nothing' would have been
pronounced more like 'no-thing'.
A 'prick-song' was a song about
fucking. 'Notes' also meant male
genitals, and long and short notes
referred to penis size}

Peter Hall's production of *Coriolanus* at the National Theatre in 1984 brought out very strongly the homoerotic nature of the relationship between Coriolanus and Aufidius. So strongly, in fact, that theatregoers in the crush bar could be heard pronouncing the play's title as 'Coriol-*anus*'.

During Shakespeare's time the theatre acquired a reputation for homosexuality. One disapproving commentator wrote that a sodomite is someone who is 'at every play and every night sups with his ingles' (an 'ingle' was the young passive partner in a homosexual relationship). In *Poetaster* (1601), a comedy by Shakespeare's fellow dramatist Ben Jonson, a father is appalled to learn that his son wants to be an actor:

*'What? Shall I have my son a stager now, an ingle for players?'*

# THINGS THAT GO THUMP IN THE NIGHT

## OTHELLO

### *Act 3, Scene 3*

The squalid language of the malignant Iago plays an important part in expressing the play's underlying theme: *Othello* is about the banality of evil, and that's what makes it such a terrifying play. Iago's concerns are the tawdry, petty, commonplace preoccupations of a little man with – we are led to assume – a little prick, who destroys lives so he can feel powerful.

Part of Iago's brilliant strategy to destroy Othello is the following false account of Cassio dreaming of making love to Desdemona. What Iago's story really reveals is his own desire for Cassio, Desdemona, and perhaps, for Othello too. But it can also be read as Iago jerking himself off.

This speech was omitted in 19th- and early 20th-century acting editions of the play.

*Iago* I lay with Cassio lately,

And being troubled with a raging tooth,

I could not sleep. There are a kind of men

So loose of soul that in their sleeps

Will mutter their affairs. One of this kind is Cassio.

In sleep I heard him say 'Sweet Desdemona,

Let us be wary, let us hide our loves',

And then, sir, would he grip and wring my hand,

Cry 'O, sweet creature!', then kiss me hard,

As if he plucked kisses by the roots,

That grew upon my lips, lay his leg o'er my thigh,

And sigh, and kiss, and then cry 'Cursèd fate,

That gave thee to the Moor!'

*Othello* O, monstrous, monstrous!

... I'll tear her all to pieces.

*Iago* I lay with Cassio recently, and being kept awake
with a throbbing prick, I couldn't sleep. There are some
men who just can't control themselves in their sleep.
They'll mutter their secret desires. Cassio's like that. In
his sleep I heard him say, 'Sweet Desdemona, we must

be careful, we must hide our love.' And then, sir, he would grip my cock and wring it, and cry out: 'O, sweet whore!' then kiss me hard, as if he was plucking kisses by the root, tearing at the hairs on my arse. He would fuck me, and sigh and kiss, and then cry out: 'Cursed fate, that gave you to the Moor!'

*Othello* O monstrous. She's made me a cuckold. I'll tear her cunt to pieces.

Raging tooth. Throbbing cock.

Hand. Cock. {A frequent pun: 'the bawdy hand of the dial is now upon the prick of noon', *Romeo and Juliet*, 2.4. 'Noon' refers to the height of an erect penis}

Creature. Whore, sodomite. {The word 'creature' is used by several male characters in Shakespeare when they accuse a woman of adultery}

Kiss. To fuck. {A term in billiards denoting the brushing of one ball against another}

Lay a leg over. To fuck.

Thigh. A general word for an area of sexual pleasure such as the vagina or backside.

Monstrous. A cuckold. {'Monstrous' also suggests same-sex desire and castration. 'Monster' was also used in a negative sense for a hermaphrodite - someone who has both male and female sex-organs}

Pieces. Punning on 'piece of flesh' to suggest whore's flesh. {'Piece' can also mean whore: in *Troilus and Cressida*, 4.1, Helen of Troy is called a 'flat tamed piece' with 'whorish loins'}

*Pertaining to*

# BROTHELS

# GET THEE TO A NUNNERY AND A WHOREHOUSE

## HAMLET

### Act 3, Scene 1

Hamlet's a callous bastard. His brutal assassination of his girlfriend's character is a particularly unsettling example of the kind of male aggression that portrays all women as whores.

In performance, this scene should be harrowing for the audience to witness. Hamlet's vicious cruelty towards a woman he once loved has a strange effect on us, alienating us from a hero for whom we would normally expect to have feelings of empathy.

Such are the complexities that make *Hamlet* the pre-eminent drama it is. Shakespeare rarely deals in one-note characters. Hamlet is painfully torn between his love for Ophelia and his disgust for all women, caused by his revulsion at his mother's sexual relations with Claudius, the uncle who has murdered his father. At this point in the play, Hamlet has just delivered his famous 'To be, or not to be' speech, in which he contemplates suicide.

*Hamlet*  I did love you once.

*Ophelia*  Indeed, my lord, you made me believe so.

*Hamlet*  You should not have believed me . . . I loved you not.

*Ophelia* I was the more deceived.

*Hamlet* Get thee to a nunnery. Why wouldst thou be a breeder of sinners? . . . We are arrant knaves, all. Believe none of us. Go thy ways to a nunnery . . .

Get thee to a nunnery, go, farewell. Or if thou wilt needs marry, marry a fool; for wise men know well enough what monsters you make of them. To a nunnery, go, and quickly, too. Farewell.

*Ophelia* O heavenly powers, restore him!

*Hamlet* You jig, you amble, and you lisp . . . and make your wantonness your ignorance. Go to, I'll no more on't. It hath made me mad . . . To a nunnery, go.

{*Exit Hamlet*}

*Hamlet* I did love you once.

*Ophelia* When we made love, my lord, you made me believe so.

*Hamlet* You should not have believed me. I loved you not.

*Ophelia* I was the more deceived then.

*Hamlet* Get yourself to a convent. Why would you want to be a breeder of sinners? We men are downright shits, all of us. Believe none of us. Fuck off to a whore-house.

**Hamlet** Get yourself to a brothel, go fuck yourself, farewell. Or if you have to marry, marry a fool, for wise men know well enough what cuckolds you whores make of them. Go and fuck off to a whorehouse, go on, go and have a quick fuck.

**Ophelia** O please God restore his sanity!

**Hamlet** You flaunt yourself in a fuck-me dance, you walk the street like a whore, you talk dirty like a prostitute, acting dumb, pretending you don't realise you're cock-teasing. Go off and fuck. I'll have no more of your sexy come-ons. It's got me aroused. To a whorehouse go, go off and fuck there.

*{Exit Hamlet}*

Indeed. Making love; sexual intercourse. {'To do' means 'to fuck'}
Nunnery. Brothel.
Monsters. Cuckolds. {The word also means homosexual, and hermaphrodite, a being who has male and female sexual elements}
Quickly. Punning on 'quick-lay', in the sense of 'quick fuck'.

Jig. A ribald song with sexually provocative dancing to accompany it.
Amble. To walk the streets soliciting for trade like a whore.
Lisp. To talk dirty.
Wantonness. Cock-teasing.
Go. To fuck.
Mad. Sexually aroused.

There are still editors of the play who insist that Hamlet's use of the word 'nunnery' means only a convent. But this is to ignore the sort of language that Hamlet has used when he described Ophelia to Polonius as 'breeding maggots in the sun', and the obscenities he will use in the next scene (see page 69), where his words to her blatantly pun on her cunt.

To a practising dramatist, rather than a scholar, it seems that Shakespeare is showing a divided self speaking here. The part of Hamlet that still loves Ophelia is urging her to go to a convent to preserve her chastity so she'll not breed sinners like him; the other part of him, the part that is repelled by her because she is a woman, like his mother, is treating her like a whore in a brothel who wants to fuck men indiscriminately.

This scene is a masterly example of how, in Shakespeare's hands, the sexual pun can express profound and complex feeling. Later, when Ophelia comes on stage with her mind torn apart, she sings bawdy songs about sex and pricks, including a refrain of a repeated 'nony', meaning vagina. When she sings 'Before you tumbled me, / You promised me to wed' – is she referring to Hamlet? We do not know.

# THE CARDINAL'S HAT: ITS TIP AFLAME WITH PROMISE

## HENRY VI, PART ONE

### Act 1, Scene 4

Shakespeare's plays abound with puns on brothels, particularly those that lined Bankside on land leased by the Bishop of Winchester between London Bridge and the Rose and Globe theatres.

Not only does Shakespeare make the earlier Bishop of Winchester (later a Cardinal) a major character in *Henry VI, Part One*, he also specifically alludes to the whores who were operating on the current Bishop's land – 'Winchester's geese' (a phrase also used to describe swellings in the groin caused by venereal disease, or victims of it), and to a notorious brothel called 'The Cardinal's Hat' (named after the colour of the tip of an erect penis). Shakespeare is here savagely satirising the present Bishop and the hypocrisy of a religious cleric who grows fat on the rents of sin.

The play opens with the quarrels of the nobles – as so often in Shakespeare, the brutality of the sexual wordplay underlines the viciousness of power politics. Here the Duke of Gloucester, who has seized power because the king is a child and too young to reign, confronts his bitter rival Winchester.

*Gloucester*  Thou that giv'st whores indulgences to sin . . .
I'll canvas thee in thy broad cardinal's hat,
If thou proceed in this thy insolence –
*Winchester*  Nay, stand thou back! I will not budge
a foot . . .

> {*Gloucester, Winchester and their men all draw their swords*}

*Gloucester*  Under my feet I'll stamp thy cardinal's hat.
In spite of Pope, or dignities of church,
Here by the cheeks I'll drag thee up and down . . .
Winchester goose! . . . Out, cloakèd hypocrite!

> {*They fight again*}

*Winchester*  Abominable Gloucester, guard thy head,
For I intend to have it ere long.

*Gloucester*  You that give whores permission to sin, I'll be
your pimp and sell you and your engorged prick if you
continue with this insolence.
*Winchester*  Just you dare! I'll not bugger and fuck
for you.

> {*Gloucester, Winchester and their men all draw their swords*}

*Gloucester* I'll stamp your whorish cock under my feet, in spite of the Pope or the fact that you're a churchman. I'll drag you up and down the street by the arse like a whore soliciting and wanking.

... Winchester whore! Go fuck yourself, you whoremonger hypocrite!

{*They fight again*}

*Winchester* Arse-fucker Gloucester, guard your head, because I intend to have it before long.

Indulgences to sin. Gloucester is referring to the profits earned by the Bishop of Winchester from the brothels on Bankside - land for which he owned the lease. {Also a pun on the church's practice of selling indulgences, or pardons, for sins}

Canvas. The implication is that Gloucester will hawk Winchester through the streets as if he were a whore.

Cardinal's Hat. The name of a notorious brothel on Bankside, named for the colour of the tip of an engorged penis.

Budge. To bugger.

Foot. Punning on French *foutre*, to fuck.

Cardinal's Hat. Cock. {Gloucester is again alluding to Winchester's hypocrisy}

Up and down. To walk up and down like a whore soliciting for trade; to rub up and down as in masturbation.

Winchester goose. Whore in one of the Bankside brothels under the jurisdiction of the Bishop of Winchester.

Out! Go fuck yourself!

Cloakèd hypocrite! A whoremonger

dressed in bishop's robes. Abominable. Arse-licking, sodomitical. {'Abominable' was also a reference to bestiality; the word was (wrongly) believed to derive from the Latin *ab homine*, 'inhuman', 'beastly'}

The great actor Edward Alleyn, who belonged to a rival theatre company to Shakespeare's, had financial interests in the brothels of Bankside. It is believed his wife Joan was a brothel bawd like Shakespeare's Mistress Quickly. She is certainly known to have been paraded in an open cart through the streets of Southwark, the 'shaming ritual' imposed as a punishment on prostitutes at the time. Alleyn himself apparently had meals with business associates in the Cardinal's Hat brothel.

# A VIRGIN TO THE HIGHEST BIDDER

## PERICLES

## *Act 2, Scene 4*

Shakespeare's depiction of a world of pimps, bawds and brothels in *Pericles* is not entirely comic. Like the play in general, it has an unsettling undercurrent.

*Pericles* is a fairy-story with a dark heart, featuring incest, shipwreck, baffling riddles, daring escapes from death and loved ones believed dead. But the virtuous actions of a young woman, Marina, will turn loss and separation and tragedy into joyful resolution. Marina's virtue does not mean 'chastity' in the literal sense of technical virginity. In Shakespeare's plays chastity means something more to do with keeping steadfast one's sense of self, with keeping one's own identity intact, and virginity is a metaphor for this.

Here Marina has been taken to a brothel, much to the delight of the bawd and the pimp who'll be able to get good money for her because she's a virgin. The exchange between the brothel keepers about her 'qualities' is a scathing attack on the exploitation of women treated as commodities for sale.

✝

*Boult* Master, I have gone through for this piece you see. If you like her, so; if not, I have lost my earnest . . .

*Bawd* What's her price, Boult?

*Boult* I cannot be bated one doit of a hundred sesterces.

*Pander* ... Wife, take her in; instruct her what she has to do, that she may not be raw in her entertainment.

*Bawd* Boult, take you the marks of her, the colour of her hair, complexion, height, her age, with warrant of her virginity, and cry 'He that will give most shall have her first.' Such a maidenhead were no cheap thing, if men were as they have been ...

*Bawd* {*To Marina*} ... you shall live in pleasure.

*Marina* No.

*Bawd* Yes, indeed shall you, and taste gentlemen of all fashions. You shall fare well. You shall have the difference of all complexions. What, do you stop your ears?

*Marina* Are you a woman?

*Boult* Master, I've bargained hard for this piece of flesh you see here. If you like her, well and good; if not, I've lost the down payment I made for her.

*Bawd* What's her price, Boult?

*Boult* I cannot have her price reduced by a penny less than a hundred sesterces.

*Pander* Wife, take her in; instruct her how to fuck so

she's not inexperienced in giving sexual pleasure to our customers.

*Bawd* Boult, advertise her attractions – the colour of her hair, complexion, height, her age, with proof of her virginity. Then cry out: 'He that will pay the most will have her first.' Such a maidenhead is not cheap if men are still the way they've always been – ready to pay a premium for breaking in a virgin.

*Bawd* {*To Marina*} You shall make a living giving sexual pleasure.

*Marina* No.

*Bawd* Yes, indeed you'll soon be having sex. You'll be fucking, and tasting gentlemen of all shapes of cocks. You'll make a good whore. You'll enjoy men of all different races fucking you. Why do you stop your ears?

*Marina* I can't believe I'm hearing all this from a woman. You should be on my side.

Piece. Piece of flesh fit for selling.

Earnest. Down payment.

Sesterces. A *sestertius* was a small Roman coin worth a quarter of a *denarius*, the latter being the commonest Roman coin in circulation.

Do. To fuck.

Raw in her entertainment. Not experienced at pleasuring the brothel customers.

Pleasure. Sexual pleasure.

Indeed. In the sex-act. {'To do' means 'to fuck'}

All. Penis. {Puns on 'awl', a hole-boring tool}

Fashions. Shapes. {Puns on the Latin *fascinum*, penis}

Mistress Holland's Brothel, a famous whorehouse in Shakespeare's time, was situated on an island on the Thames. Like the theatres and brothels of Bankside, it lay outside the jurisdiction of the city authorities. It took amazing measures to protect its position. It was surrounded by a moat, complete with a drawbridge and a guard armed with a halberd (a weapon with a long shaft and axe blade and pick, topped by a spear-head). The door was heavily studded and had a special spy-hole. The garden was designed on formal lines, with paths for the whores and their customers to stroll on. And there was also an arbor in the corner of the garden for more private encounters.

*Pertaining to*

# MALE WHORE

—————————————————

—————————————————

# THE HOMOPHOBE'S BI(B)LE

## TROILUS AND CRESSIDA

### Act 5, Scene 1

Brutal sexual language is a substitute for military fighting in *Troilus and Cressida*. Shakespeare's depiction of the Trojan Wars thoroughly subverts the version of events recounted by the ancient Greek poet Homer in *The Iliad*.

Instead of an epic tale of heroic deeds and noble motives, played out in a battle between legendary warriors, Shakespeare produced a blistering satire on war, in which military honour has been emptied of all significance, martial heroism replaced by petty squabbling, and morality reduced to a question of whatever each man decides is of value. Even love is devalued, as an 'open ulcer' associated more with venereal disease than innocent desire.

The homosexual relationship of Achilles and Patroclus provides the only scenes in the play in which love is portrayed with any tenderness. The rancid-mouthed camp-follower Thersites torments them with curses on their sex life, but perhaps his outpouring of rage betrays a suspicious over-zealousness ...

{*Achilles and Patroclus lying in bed, lolling*}

*Thersites* Prithee be silent, boy ... Thou art thought to be Achilles' male varlet.

*Patroclus* 'Male varlet', you rogue? What's that?

*Thersites* Why, his masculine whore. Now the rotten diseases of the south, the guts-griping, ruptures, loads o'gravel in the back, lethargies, cold palsies, raw eyes, dirt-rotten livers, wheezing lungs, bladders full of impostume, sciaticas, lime-kilns i'th'palm, incurable boneache, and the rivelled fee-simple of the tetter, take and take again such preposterous discoveries!

*Patroclus* Why, thou damnable box of envy thou, what mean'st thou to curse thus?

*Thersites* Do I curse thee?

*Patroclus* Why, no, you ruinous butt, you whoreson indistinguishable cur, no.

*Thersites* Shut your face, you buggering boy. They call you Achilles' male harlot.

*Patroclus* You dare call me 'Male varlet', you shit? What's that?

*Thersites* Why, his masculine whore. Let every kind of cock-rotting clap, gut-wrenching spasms, hernias, agonising aches, diseased balls, impotence, cold paralysis of the cock, raw arse, dirt-rotting livers, wheezing lungs, bladders full of abscesses, sciaticas, burning of the palms, incurable syphilis and the perpetual possession of a pox-infested scabs and shrivelled-up skin, attack, and attack again, your disgusting, blatantly flaunted buggery perversions.

*Patroclus* Why, you fucking cunt of envy, you. What do you mean by cursing me like this?

*Thersites* Do I curse you?

*Patroclus* Why, no, you little shit, you envious kill-joy son-of-a-bitch, you deformed beast, no.

Boy. Buggering boy.

Varlet. Whore.

Rotten. (Cock)-rotting.

Diseases of the south. Sexually transmitted diseases, believed to have been imported from the south, particularly France and Italy.

Loads o'gravel in the back. Diseased balls. {'Loads' refers to balls and semen; 'gravel' to kidney stones}

Lethargies. Impotence, sexual inertia.

Palsies. Paralysis of the cock.

Eyes. Arse.

Sciaticas. Agonising aches, sometimes associated with sexually transmitted diseases.

Boneache. Syphilis. {The disease was sometimes called 'Neapolitan boneache' because it was thought to have been imported from Italy, and from Naples in particular}

Rivelled. Shrivelled-up.

Fee simple. Absolute possession of. {A legal term for 'perpetual ownership'}

Tetter. Syphilitic scabs.

Preposterous discoveries. Flaunted acts of buggery. {'Preposterous' puns on arse}

In a satirical book of 1609 called *The Gull's Hornbook*, addressed to gallants – the young men about town who strutted their stuff through London and went to the theatre not to enjoy a play, but to be seen and admired by other playgoers – the author advised such men to buy a good stool for sixpence when they went to the theatre because 'by sitting on the stage you may, with small cost, purchase the dear [arse] acquaintance [knowledge of their private parts] of the boys [passive male homosexuals]'.

In Thomas Middleton's *Old Father Hubbard's Tales* (1604), a lecherous young gallant is urged to call in at Blackfriars Theatre, where the boy companies performed, in the hope of seeing 'a nest of boys able to ravish a man'.

# THE POLITICAL PROSTITUTE

## HENRY VIII (ALL IS TRUE)

### Act 4, Scene 2

Shakespeare's Cardinal Wolsey whores his soul for power.
A lowly butcher's son, he has bribed and palm-greased his
way to become the most powerful man in England, wrecking
the careers of his rivals for the prize of being Henry VIII's
Lord Chancellor. But after the rise comes the fall, as Wolsey's
many enemies - those he has trampled on to get to the top -
take their revenge.

With the news of Wolsey's death, Henry VIII's first wife, Queen
Katherine, and her usher, Griffith, cast an ironic eye over the Cardinal's
career. On the surface, Griffith seems to be praising Wolsey, but this is
another example of how Shakespeare uses sexual puns to reveal the irony
of what a character is really saying. Griffith's sarcasm – communicated
through the ribald wordplay – is razor-keen.

*Katherine*  He was a man

Of an unbounded stomach . . .

He would say untruths, and be ever double

Both in his words and meaning . . .

Of his own body he was ill, and gave

The clergy ill example . . .

*Griffith*  This cardinal,

Though from an humble stock, undoubtedly

Was fashioned to much honour. From his cradle

He was a scholar, and a ripe and good one . . .

Lofty and sour to them that loved him not,

But to those men that sought him, sweet as summer.

*Katherine*  He was a man of unbounded sexual appetite.
He told lies and was always having sex with men. He
was a whore and a pander. He was sexually immoral and
gave the clergy a reputation for licentiousness.

*Griffith*  He was from humble stock, this Cardinal, but
he was ruthless in his determination to raise his cock to
potency. Right from his cradle he was a scholar of sex,
a sexually rank one, and a whore. He was aloof and sour
to those who did not love him, but to those men who
flattered him, he was sexually intimate, and lusty as
summer.

Stomach. Sexual appetite.

Double. The reference is to union with one's double, in this case homosexual union. {'Double' also meant bisexual}

Words. Whore. {Punning on the sound of 'whored'}

Meaning. Pandering. {Money earned by a pimp or from whoring}

Ill. Sexually immoral, licentious.

{'Ill' also meant unmanly}

Fashioned. A reference to 'cock'. {Punning on the Latin *fascinum*, meaning penis}

Ripe. Sexually rank.

Good one. Whore.

Lofty. The suggestion here is of a rise to potency, i.e. an erection.

Sweet. Sexually intimate.

Sir Francis Bacon, Lord Chancellor of England in Shakespeare's time, would have been chucked out of today's government for his sexual escapades. But unlike many of today's politicians, Bacon never made any secret of his sexual predilections. He was a noted sodomite. One writer at the time wrote that he was 'a pederast. His Ganymedes and Favourites took bribes: but his lordship always gave judgement according what was just and good'. But he was impeached on charges of bribery and corrupt dealings, not sodomy. His older brother Anthony was also what we now call a homosexual, and at one time was wanted in France on a charge of buggery.

# SEXUAL
# (S)WORDPLAY
## CORIOLANUS
### *Act 5, Scene 6*

Two soldiers fight over who's going to be the one to be buggered.
The relationship between the warriors Aufidius and Coriolanus
is depicted throughout the play as one between sexual partners
vying for the aggressive position.

In this, their final encounter, Aufidius dares to call Coriolanus 'boy'
(a passive homosexual). The verbal violence of the scene has an
intensity that makes it one of the most powerful in Shakespeare.

*Aufidius*  Thou boy of tears.

*Coriolanus*                    Ha?

*Aufidius*                              No more.

*Coriolanus*  Measureless liar ...

... 'Boy'? O slave! - ...

Cut me to pieces, Volsces. Men and lads,

Stain all your edges on me. 'Boy'! False hound,

If you have writ your annals true, 'tis there

That, like an eagle in a dove-cote, I

Fluttered your Volscians in Corioles.

Alone I did it. 'Boy'!

*Aufidius* You boy of tears, you bum-boy!

*Coriolanus* What was that?

*Aufidius* Forget it.

*Coriolanus* You buggered cock-less coward. You dare to

call me 'bum-boy'? O sodomite!

... Cut me to pieces, castrate me, Volsces. Men

and lads, stain all your swords with my blood, smear all

your cocks with my spunk. 'Bum boy'! False sodomite,

if you've written down the truth of what I've done, it

will say that, like an eagle, in a dove-cote, I fluttered

your Volscians in Corioles. Alone I did it. 'Bum-boy'!

Boy. Passive homosexual, bum-boy.
Measureless. With nothing to
measure, i.e. without a cock.
Liar. Bugger. {Punning on the
Italian *bugiare*, meaning to lie}
Slave. A passive homosexual,
kept for sodomy.

Cut. To castrate.
Stain. To stain with semen.
Edges. Erections. {The allusion
is to the 'edge' of a sword,
i.e. a penis}
Hound. Sodomite. {'Dog' was a
frequent term for a sodomite}

Shakespeare's friend and most formidable rival, Christopher Marlowe, was arrested on charges of atheism and blasphemy. He was accused of stating that:

> *'Christ was a bastard, and his mother was dishonest [a whore]. St John the Evangelist was bedfellow to Christ . . . and used him as the sinners of Sodoma [do]. All they that love not tobacco and boys [homosexual young men] are fools.'*

*Pertaining to*

# FEMALE WHORE

———————————

———————————

# A FATHERLY CHAT
## ROMEO AND JULIET
### *Act 3, Scene 5*

Some of the most repulsive sexual puns in Shakespeare are spoken by fathers to their daughters. The playwright reserves his most venomous bile for cruel and unforgiving fathers, and his most tender compassion for the daughters of such monsters.

Here, Juliet has told her parents she doesn't want to marry Paris, their choice of husband for her. Capulet lunges towards his only child, barely restraining his physical violence, and we look on helpless, with a mounting sense of outrage, as he screams ferocious obscenities at her.

*Capulet* Fettle your fine joints 'gainst Thursday next

To go with Paris to Saint Peter's Church,

Or I will drag thee on a hurdle thither.

Out, you green-sickness carrion! Out, you baggage,

You tallow-face! ...

*Juliet* {*kneels down*} Good father, I beseech you on my

knees,

Hear me with patience but to speak a word.

*Capulet* Hang thee, young baggage, disobedient wretch!

I tell thee what: get thee to church o' Thursday,

Or never after look me in the face.

Speak not, reply not, do not answer me.

{*Juliet rises*}

My fingers itch . . .

Out on her, hilding! . . .

Graze where you will, you shall not house with me.

. . . beg, starve, die in the streets,

For, by my soul, I'll ne'er acknowledge thee . . .

✝

*Capulet* Get your genitals ready for a thrashing on
Thursday next to go to Saint Peter's Church with Paris,
or I'll drag you there on a whore's cart. Whore! You
pox-diseased piece of dead, putrefying flesh! You whore!
You pestilent slut. You greasy-cunt!

*Juliet* {*kneels down*} Good father, I beseech you on my
knees, hear me, please be patient and let me say a word.

*Capulet* Go and act the pimp and hire yourself out,
young whore, disobedient wretch! I tell you what. Get
you to church Thursday, or never afterwards look me in
the face. Speak not, reply not, do not answer me!

{*Juliet rises*}

My fingers are itching to beat her up. Fuck her, the slag!

*Capulet* Live as a whore wherever you want to, you're not living in my house any more. Whore, starve, have sexual orgasms like a whore in the street, because by my soul, I'll disown you, I'll never acknowledge you again!

Fettle. Get ready. {'Fettle' also means to thrash or beat. It puns here on sexual intercourse}

Joints. Genitals.

Hurdle. Cart that led prostitutes through the streets to shame them. {Capulet may be referring to St Katherine's reform house for fallen girls in London}

Green-sickness. The pox,

syphilis. {See below}

Carrion. Piece of putrefying flesh.

Baggage. Whore.

Hilding. Slag.

Graze. To be a whore. {A pun on the services provided by a shepherd in return for free grazing for his sheep}

Beg. To whore.

Die. A frequent pun on orgasm.

The word 'greensickness' can refer to the anaemia suffered by young, newly menstruating women, which was believed in Shakespeare's time to be cured by sexual satisfaction. But Capulet is here using the word in its other sense of syphilis. Through the pun, and by drawing attention to Juliet's tender age (her 'green-sickness'), Shakespeare reinforces the cruelty of her father's treatment of her.

Unless we understand the full scope of the sexual subtext of Capulet's language, we cannot grasp the harrowing impact that the scene is designed to have on the audience. This is one among many examples in Shakespeare where productions often fail fully to capture the shocking nature of a scene, and thereby deprive audiences of their true – and terrifying – effect.

Shakespeare's disgust at the way fathers assume rights over the bodies of their daughters, expressed in the coarse sexual puns he gives them to say, runs through his plays as a recurring strand. He himself had two daughters.

# STRETCHING THE VELVET

## HENRY VIII (ALL IS TRUE)

### Act 2, Scene 3

A cynical old whore at the court of Henry VIII gives the King's future wife Anne Boleyn some advice. Henry has his sights set on Anne, but first he will have to divorce his first wife, Katherine of Aragon.

Male characters in *Henry VIII* describe Anne as 'an angel' and praise her 'beauty and honour'. But Shakespeare subverts the image of her as a chaste young woman by having her exchange ribald puns with men early on in the play. The old whore thinks Anne's a slut, and accuses her of hypocrisy. The ribald puns on Henry's cock are deliberately silly and comic.

✝

*Anne* By my troth and maidenhead,

I would not be a queen.

*Old Lady* Beshrew me, I would –

And venture maidenhead for't; and so would you,

For all this spice of your hypocrisy.

You, that have so fair parts of woman on you,

. . . and which gifts,

Saving your mincing, the capacity

Of your soft cheveril conscience would receive

If you might please to stretch it.

*Anne*  Nay, good troth.

*Old Lady*  Yes, troth and troth. You would not be

a queen? . . .

        {*Enter Lord Chamberlain*}

*Lord Chamberlain* . . . Perceive I speak sincerely, and

high note's

Ta'en of your many virtues, the King's majesty

Commends his good opinion of you and

Does purpose honour to you no less flowing

Than Marchioness of Pembroke; to which title

A thousand pound a year annual support

Out of his grace he adds.

*Anne*  On my faith and virginity I would not be

a queen.

*Old Lady*  Devil take me, I would - and prostitute my

virginity for it. And so would you however much you

say you wouldn't - your hypocritical affectation is a

pose. Your soft pliant cunt you call your conscience

would receive great gifts if you decided to stretch it by having sex.

*Anne* No, old whore.

*Old Lady* Yes, slut, and you'll play the whore. You're not telling me you don't want to be queen?

{*Enter Lord Chamberlain*}

*Lord Chamberlain* I hope you realise that I speak sincerely. Having taken note of your many virtues, the King's majesty commends his sexually virile prick to you and intends to sexually probe and present you with no less copious an honour than Marchioness of Pembroke. In addition to this title, he gives you, out of the generosity of his cock, a thousand pound a year anal support for you so you can bear his arse in the sex act.

Queen. Whore. {Often spelled as 'quean'}

Venture. To prostitute.

Cheveril. Cunt. {A reference to kid leather, which stretches easily}

Troth. Whore. {'Trot' was a 16th-century word for a prostitute}

Good opinion. Sexually virile prick. {A 'pinion' was a feather, a punning word for penis}

Purpose. Intend, probe sexually.

Title. Prick and arse.

Annual. Relating to the anus.

Support. To bear a sexual partner's weight in the sex act.

Grace. Cock. {Punning on the Greek *charis*, 'grace', and *keros*, 'horn'}

Cheveril was very fine kidskin that was pliant and easily stretched. Shakespeare often uses gloves and leather as metaphors for skin stretching in sexual movement. His father, John Shakespeare, bought and sold leather and wool, as well as working as a glover, and it seems likely Shakespeare would have helped in his workshop.

# THE CROSS-DRESSED QUEEN

## HENRY VI, PART THREE

### Act 1, Scene 4

A complex, blood-soaked drama spanning ten years of the 15th-century Wars of the Roses, *Henry VI, Part Three* is punctuated by battles and strewn with corpses - both Lancastrian and Yorkist. The play is dominated by a brutal adulteress with a taste for battle. Queen Margaret, the French wife of the Lancastrian King Henry VI, is a brilliant general; as a mother she is utterly ruthless in her efforts to win back her son's right to the throne from the Duke of York.

After she has won the Battle of Wakefield, during which York's son Rutland is gratuitously butchered by Lord Clifford, Margaret offers a handkerchief to the captured father to wipe away his tears of grief, telling him that it has been dipped in the blood of his son. No wonder he calls her a poisonous whore.

*York* She-wolf of France, but worse than wolves

of France,

Whose tongue more poisons than the adder's tooth -

How ill-beseeming is it in thy sex

To triumph like an Amazonian trull ...

O tiger's heart wrapped in a woman's hide!

*York* Whore of France, but who whores more than all the whores of France, whose clitoris is more poisonous than the adder's tooth!

How unbecoming is it in your sex to triumph like an Amazonian, masculine slag. You cunt, you tiger's heart wrapped in a whore's cunt!

She-wolf. Whore.

Worse. Punning on 'whores'.

Tongue. Clitoris.

Amazons. Legendary race of female warriors who governed themselves and lived apart from men. They were thought to have cut off their right breasts to improve their aim in archery. They were often associated in Shakespeare's time with female transvestites. {*Amazone* was a French term for a riding habit and carried the suggestion of both huntress and sexual predator}

Trull. Prostitute, slag.

O. Cunt. {The letter 'O' puns on the female genitals, as do certain other words for circular or ring-like objects}

Tiger. A man-like woman. Also a eunuch or homosexual.

Woman's hide. Whore's cunt. {Hide is 'leather', a word that denoted both 'cunt' and 'whore'}

Shakespeare took London by storm with *Henry VI, Part Three* – and incurred the jealousy of other playwrights like Robert Greene, who, in *A Groatsworth of Wit* (1592), calls Shakespeare a castrated whore:

> '*An upstart Crow [a cocky new boy on the block with ideas above his station] . . . his Tiger's [eunuch's] heart wrapt in a Player's hide [in whorish flesh], supposes he is as well able to bombast out blank verse as the best of you: and being an absolute Johannes factotum [jack⸗of⸗all⸗trades], is in his own conceit the only Shakes⸗scene in a country.*'

We don't know whether Shakespeare responded directly to the insult in print, but his audiences then and since certainly did so for him. Who's ever heard of Robert Greene?

*Pertaining to*

# THE CLAP

—————————————

—————————————

# MURDER MOST FOUL

## HAMLET

### Act 1, Scene 5

Syphilis snakes its pestilent way through *Hamlet* like a running sore. Images of sex as disease - flesh crusted with scabs, a body burning with raging boils, sheets smeared by the incestuous exchange of semen, a young virgin breeding maggots in the sun. And threaded through the play alongside these are images of impotence caused by unnatural sexual acts. This is how Shakespeare conveys the corruption and sleaze of the Danish court under the rule of Hamlet's uncle, Claudius, who has murdered his father and married his mother.

When Hamlet cries out 'There is something rotten in the state of Denmark', 'rotten' means 'venereally infected'. 'State', another term for 'throne', puns on the arse and its stool (shit). Hamlet is saying that Denmark's a pox-infested pit of shit, evacuated from Claudius' bowels.

Here, in the first act of the play, his father's Ghost tells Hamlet how he was murdered by his own brother. He charges his son to take revenge.

> *Ghost* Revenge {thy dear father's} foul and most
> unnatural murder.
>
> *Hamlet* Murder?
>
> *Ghost* Murder most foul ...

*Ghost* ... Upon my secure hour thy uncle stole
With juice of cursèd hebenon in a vial,
And in the porches of mine ears did pour
The leperous distilment, whose effect
Holds such an enmity with blood of man
That swift as quicksilver it courses through
The natural gates and alleys of the body,
And with a sudden vigour it doth posset
And curd, like eager droppings into milk,
The thin and wholesome blood. So did it mine;
And a most instant tetter barked about,
Most lazar-like, with vile and loathsome crust,
All my smooth body.

*Ghost* Revenge your dear father's foul and most
unnatural murder.

*Hamlet* Murder?

*Ghost* Murder most foul. Your uncle stole up to me,
holding a vial of the poison henbane, and poured it into
my ears – it was a syphilis-causing distillation, which has
a murdering toxic effect when mixed with the blood of
manhood. Swift as mercury, as it courses through the
sexual organs – the gates and alleys – of the body,

it instantly curdles the semen with powerful force - like acid dropping into milk. So in the same way, this poison dropped into my thin and wholesome semen. Immediately, vile and loathsome venereal crusts like a leper's spread all over my smooth body.

Leprous. Causing syphilis.

Man. Manhood.

Quicksilver. Mercury.

{For centuries mercury was used as a 'treatment' for syphilis. See also below}

Natural gates and alleys. Sex organs.

Blood. Semen.

Tetter. Venereal scab.

The plays of the time are full of references to 'cures' for syphilis, none of which can have had any beneficial effect. The illustration on the frontispiece of *Cornelianum Dolium*, an anonymous contemporary comedy in Latin, shows a syphilis sufferer in a sweating-tub. The inscription on the tub reads: 'I sit on the throne of love, I suffer in the tub.' The speech bubble coming from his mouth says: 'Farewell, O sexual pleasures and lusts.'

In *All's Well That Ends Well*, the brutish Bertram – one of Shakespeare's most repulsive characters – is described as having infected an Italian girl with the French pox (syphilis). His reference to his 'sick desires' (4.2) may well be an allusion to the contemporary belief that sex with a virgin could heal a man's syphilis – the disease being thought to pass from the man to the virgin.

# A VENEREAL
# WHEEZE

## TROILUS AND CRESSIDA

### *Act 5, Scene 11*

To judge from the plays of Shakespeare and his contemporaries, it would seem that the whole of London suffered from the clap. References to venereal disease and its various treatments abound in the drama of the time.

*Troilus and Cressida* is particularly rich in references to sexually transmitted diseases. Here, the cynical Pandarus, whose very name means 'pimp', turns to the audience at the very end of the play and puts on us a very uncomfortable-making curse. If he's got to suffer the torment of the pox, he's going to make damned sure we will too.

*Pandarus*  My fear is this:

Some galled goose of Winchester would hiss.

Till then I'll sweat and seek about for eases,

And at that time bequeath you my diseases.

*Pandarus*  My fear is this: some sore-encrusted, diseased whore in the audience will want to hiss me and wheeze her pox all over me. Till then I'll sit in the sweating-tub and search for remedies to cure me. And then I'll bequeath you my venereal diseases.

Gallèd. Covered in venereal sores.

Goose of Winchester. Whore. {The Bishop of Winchester was the landlord of many brothels on Bankside, which provided him with a very lucrative income; see also page 192}

Hiss. A wheeze caused by venereal disease.

Sweat. A reference to the sweating-tubs in which sufferers from syphilis sat in the hope of 'steaming out' the disease.

Diseases. All venereal diseases.

The English language of Shakespeare's day boasted a considerable variety of terms for venereal diseases. Many of these reflected the xenophobic idea that such diseases were an unwanted foreign import. It's not surprising that the countries credited with bringing venereal infection into the country were England's traditional enemies.

'Malady of France' was a term for syphilis. 'French crown', a term for a bald head, alluded to the syphilis sufferers going bald. 'Piled for a French velvet' meant infected with a sexually transmitted disease. 'Neapolitan bone-ache', another term for syphilis, blamed the disease on the Italians. The English also believed that Italians were exceptionally lecherous and fond of unorthodox coital positions.

# ON DEATH ROW

## MEASURE FOR MEASURE

### *Act 3, Scene 1*

Brothels, whores, pimps and plenty of doses of the clap feature in *Measure for Measure*, a play that explores what happens when a government attempts to control people's sexuality. The Duke of Vienna decides to outlaw prostitution and to resurrect an old law making sex before marriage punishable by death.

Claudio, arrested under the new law because his girlfriend is pregnant, is about to have his head chopped off, even though the pair have a legal pre-marriage contract which meant they were, to all intents and purposes, legally married. The Duke, who is too cowardly to enforce the law himself, has given the task to his deputy. Disguised as a friar, the Duke visits Claudio in prison and accuses him of having VD. He describes the tormenting pain of the disease – a pain so agonising that even the young man's balls will cry out for death in order to be put out of their misery. He's just the kind of visitor that an innocent young father-to-be on death row needs to cheer him up . . .

*Duke*  Be absolute for death . . .

. . . Friend hast thou none,

For thine own bowels, which do call thee sire,

The mere effusion of thy proper loins,

Do curse the gout, serpigo, and the rheum,

For ending thee no sooner.

*Duke* Make up your mind to die. You have no friends. Your own balls, which call you father, the lecherous semen of your own loins, yes, your own balls curse your venereal disease, the syphilitic sores, and the gonorrhoea, for not ending your life sooner.

Mere. Lecherous. {Punning on 'merrily' for 'lustily'}

Effusion. Semen.

Gout. Venereal disease. {'French gout' was another contemporary

term for such diseases. See also page 230}

Serpigo. Disfiguring syphilitic sores on the skin.

Rheum. Gonorrhoea.

Shakespeare would have been reflecting on his own marriage when he wrote *Measure for Measure*. When he married Anne Hathaway, she was more than three months pregnant. During the 19th century a document was discovered dated 28 November 1582 and relating to the speeding up of the wedding of '"William Shagspere" and "Anne Hathwey" of Stratford in the diocese of Worcester, maiden.' The pair were issued with their marriage licence in haste, after only one reading of the banns instead of the usual three. Friends of Anne's father bought a special 'pre-contract' (of the kind that Claudio and Juliet have in *Measure for Measure*), for a staggering £40 (in those days the annual salary of a schoolmaster was £15). Some historians argue that the tradition of 'plighting a troth' permitted the delightfully termed 'fleshly meddling' before the sacred vows were made. Will and Anne's daughter Susanna was baptised six months after their wedding.

# Pertaining to
# DILDOS

# THE EVER-READY PARTNER

## THE WINTER'S TALE

*Act 4, Scene 4*

Dildos were a hot topic in Shakespeare's time because their excessive use was associated with unusually large clitorises – all that rubbing! Men feared women's use of dildos for obvious reasons. As instruments of women's pleasure dildos have distinct advantages over a real penis. A dildo is light, doesn't flop, stands stiff, is ready and waiting whenever the inclination arises, and, best of all, never gets a girl pregnant. And there is none of that messy premature ejaculation to mop up . . .

Plenty of plays and poems refer to these ingenious devices, often barely disguising male anxieties at being upstaged by a pleasure-giver that could give 100 per cent satisfaction. The one quality that men seemed to resent more than others was that these upstarts never suffered from the dreaded droop.

In *The Winter's Tale*, Autolycus, swindler, pickpocket and pedlar, and a great Shakespearean comic character with a fine line in crude innuendo, arrives in Bohemia to sell his wares and ballads. There's much bawdy play on his ribbons, gloves, and songs, particularly his 'dildos' – indelicate refrains of ballads. He also sells substitutes for erect penises made of leather, wax or glass. Was this the original advertisement for the ultimate in sex toys for women and men?

✝

*Servant* He hath songs for man or woman, of all sizes. No milliner can so fit his customers with gloves. He has the prettiest love songs for maids ... with such delicate burdens of dildos and fadings, 'Jump her, and thump her' ...

*Autolycus* {*singing*}

Pins and poking-sticks of steel,
What maids lack from head to heel
Come buy ...

✝

*Servant* He has dildos for man or woman, of all sizes for all shapes of genitals and arses. No glove-maker can bring a female prostitute or male brothel-goer so quickly to orgasm with his gloves. He has the sexiest dildos for virgins, such lightweight burdens of sensual dildos and refrains that sound like orgasms: 'Jump into her and fuck her.'

*Autolycus* {*singing*} Pricks and poking-sticks of steel, everything maids need from penis tip to heel. Come and buy.

Song. A Fuck. {'To sing' is a pun on 'to fuck'}

Sizes. The reference is to the dimensions of genitals and arses.

Milliner. Glover.

Fit. The reference is to sex-organs 'fitting'; also to orgasm, and sexual intercourse.

Customers. Brothel-goers.

Prettiest. Sexiest. {'Pretty action' was a phrase denoting sexual activity}

Delicate. Lightweight, voluptuous. {A contrast is implied between the lightness of a dildo and the heavy weight of a partner pressing down on top of a lover}

Dildos. Ballad refrains, punning on the sex-aids.

Fadings. Orgasms.

Jump. To thrust into athletically.

Pins. Pricks.

Poking sticks. Pricks.

Head. Tip of the penis, foreskin.

In *The Choice of Valentines* by Thomas Nashe, a woman tells her lover that he's lousy in bed. His prick keeps going limp, making him totally unreliable when it comes to pleasuring her. So she's got herself a more dependable partner. It is such a cruel put-down of her man's masculinity you can't help feeling sorry for him. And perhaps worst of all, the woman addresses her new sex toy not with the neutral 'it' but with 'he'!

And let's not forget – this poem was written by a man. Was Nashe writing from personal experience?

> 'Henceeforth no more will I implore thine aid . . .
> My little dildo shall supply their kind.
> A knave that moves as light as leaves by wind;
> That bendeth not, nor fouled any deal,
> But stands as stiff, as he were made of steel
> And plays at peacock twixt my legs right blithe,
> And doeth my tickling swaze with many a sigh;
> And never make my tender bellie swell.'

# PUTTING ON THE DICKS

## THE MERCHANT OF VENICE

### Act 3, Scene 4

When Shakespeare's crossed-dressed women talk about adopting the behaviour and gestures of a man it is usually as a send-up of men's self-regarding conceit and/or pomposity. Here Portia, the heroine of *The Merchant of Venice*, and her gentlewoman, Nerissa, dress up as a lawyer and clerk.

Portia says she'll have to look the part – by adding a false penis to her costume. Nerissa worries that they will actually turn into men and use their dildos to fuck women.

> *Portia* They shall think we are accomplishèd
> With that we lack. I'll hold thee any wager,
> When we are both accoutered like young men
> I'll prove the prettier fellow of the two,
> And wear my dagger with the braver grace,
> And speak between the change of man and boy
> With a reed voice, and turn two mincing steps
> Into a manly stride, and speak of frays

Like a fine bragging youth, and tell quaint lies
How honourable ladies sought my love,
Which I denying, they fell sick and died ...
*Nerissa*  Why, shall we turn to men?
*Portia*  Fie, what a question's that
If thou wert near a lewd interpreter!
But come, I'll tell thee all my whole device
When I am in my coach ...

*Portia*  They'll think we're equipped with pricks which
we haven't got. I bet you anything when we're both
dressed like young men, I'll prove the sexier of the two,
and wear my false penis with its most fine erection.
I'll certainly be well-hung. I'll turn two mincing steps
into a manly stride, and speak of sexual conquests like a
youth talking out of his arse, all cock and codpiece, and
tell quaint lies about the cunts of chaste ladies who
wanted to make love to me. Ladies who, when I turned
down their advances, crouched down and begged to be
fucked.
*Nerissa*  What, shall we turn into men and fuck
women?

*Portia* Don't be stupid! What sort of a question is that? You're talking like a greasy interpreter! But come on, I'll show you all of my vagina and my dildo when I get into in the privacy of my coach.

Prettier. Sexier. {'Pretty' means 'sexual'}

Dagger. Dildo, false penis.

Grace Penis. [Punning on the Greek *charis*, 'grace', and *keros*, 'horn'}

Frays. Sexual conquests, deflowering of virgins.

Fine. Arse. {'Fine' meant end}

Brag. Cock and codpiece. {The French word *braguette* meant codpiece – and also what was inside it}

Quaint. Cunt. {More than two centuries before, the word was used by Chaucer, best known for his bawdy *Canterbury Tales*: 'And prively he caughte hire by the queynte'}

Fall sick. To crouch for intercourse.

Die. To reach orgasm.

Turn to men. To turn into men and fuck women.

Lewd. Greasy, filthy.

All. Penis. {Punning on 'awl', a boring-tool; and also on 'hole' in the sense of 'vagina'}

Whole. Hole, vagina.

Device. Dildo.

A play by one of Shakespeare's fellow dramatists contained a refrain in which the female singer addresses the dildo as it does its work. As she plays with her sex toy, she sings to it: 'Dildido dildido / Oh love, oh love / I feel thy rage romble below and above' ('I feel your erection throbbing passionately in my vagina and my mouth').

# *Pertaining to*
# B O O B S

# A HOT COCK GONE COLD

## HENRY IV, PART ONE

*Act 2, Scene 4*

Hotspur's name means both 'hot cock' and 'tosspot'. But he hasn't been using his cock much lately, and his wife has got suspicious because he doesn't want to have sex with her any more.

In one of the most realistic scenes of marital quarrelling in Shakespeare, she complains that instead of fulfilling his conjugal duties, he's been muttering about war and battles in his sleep. When she confronts him with her hunch that he's having an affair, he replies in riddles.

*Lady Percy* Out, you mad-headed ape!

A weasel hath not such a deal of spleen

As you are tossed with.

In faith, I'll know your business, Harry, that I will . . .

Come, come, you paraquito, answer me

Directly to this question that I ask.

In faith, I'll break thy little finger, Harry,

An if thou wilt not tell me all things true.

*Hotspur*  Away, away, you trifler! Love? I love thee not.
I care not for thee, Kate. This is no world
To play with maumets and to tilt with lips.
We must have bloody noses and cracked crowns ...

*Lady Percy*  Get away with you, you hot-tipped penis!
You lecherous monkey! A weasel doesn't have such a
load of spunk as you are tossed with. I'm telling you, I'll
know what sexual exploits you've been up to, Harry,
believe me.
Come, have an orgasm, fuck me, you little parrot. I'm
telling you, I'll break your little prick, Harry, if you
won't tell me the truth. You've got to tell me everything.
*Hotspur*  Fuck off, fuck off, stop wasting time on petty
things.
Love? I love you not. I don't care for you, Kate. This is
no time to play with breasts and thrust into vaginas.
We've got to shed our spunk and crack the the hymens
of virgins {i.e. go to war}.

Mad-headed. Mad with desire. {The reference is to a penis-head hot with lust}

Ape. Monkeys were considered excessively lecherous.

Weasel. The folk-song 'Pop Goes the Weasel' refers to the animal's frequent explosion of semen in ejaculation.

Spleen. Spunk.

Come. Reach orgasm.

Answer. To thrust, to fuck. {From a fencing term for a return hit}

Finger. Prick.

Away. Fuck off!

Maumets. Breasts.

Tilt. To thrust into.

Lips. Vaginal lips.

Bloody. The reference is to blood in the sense of semen.

Nose. Penis.

Crack. To break the hymen.

Crown. Virginal membrane, hymen.

A statue of a woman 'for the most part naked, with Thames-water (s)pilling from her breasts'. This is how the chronicler John Stow described in his *Survey of London* of 1603 a fountain that had recently been built in the Westcheap part of London. The centrepiece of this fountain was a statue of Diana, goddess of Chastity.

In *As You Like It*, 4.1, the heroine Rosalind, disguised as a boy, Ganymede (i.e. homosexual), tells the man she loves that when s/he marries, she will be more 'giddy in my [sexual] desires than a monkey' and that she 'will weep for nothing, like Diana in the fountain, and I will do that when you're disposed to be merry' (when you're feeling horny). Since Rosalind/Ganymede talks of nothing but sex in this speech, s/he is clearly being ironic when she refers to the fountain of the goddess of Chastity. There were several of these fountains in London.

# SHE WAS
# ASKING FOR IT

## THE RAPE OF LUCRECE

*Lines 407–417*

Shakespeare takes the story of one of the most famous rapes in history and turns it into a brilliant, complex exploration of the psychology of violence towards women. He depicts rape not solely as a matter of lust, but also of violence, and the use of power, physical and mental, over the victim.

The rape of Lucretia by Tarquin, the son of the King of Rome, that took place in 509 BC, was well known to Shakespeare's audiences. Having revealed Tarquin's crime to her relatives and begged them to take revenge, Lucretia committed suicide. Her family exhibited her corpse in the Roman Forum, and, following a mass revolt, the Tarquins were forced into exile.

The poem's condemnation of Tarquin's moral cowardice is reinforced by giving him the traditional male rapist's excuse. 'The fault is thine. For those thine eyes betray thee unto mine.' In other words, 'She was asking for it.'

✝

Her breasts like ivory globes circled with blue,

A pair of maiden worlds unconquerèd,

Save of their lord no bearing yoke they knew,

And him by oath they truly honourèd.

These worlds in Tarquin new ambition bred . . .
What could he see but mightily he noted?
What did he note but strongly he desired?
What he beheld, on that he firmly doted,
And in his will his wilful eye he tired.

Her breasts are like ivory globes circled with blue veins,
a pair of virgin worlds unconquered, that had never been
touched by any man apart from her husband.
And Lucrece had sworn that her breasts would be
possessed only by her husband. The sight of her breasts
stirred renewed lust in Tarquin. Whatever he set his
eyes on, his penis was madly aroused. Whatever he
gazed on, he strongly desired. Whatever he looked on,
made his cock swell hard, and whatever he saw, his
lecherous cock fed hungrily on.

Circled with blue. Circled with blue veins.

Maiden. Virgin.

New ambition bred. Bred renewed lust in him.

Noted. Sexually aroused. {Punning on the 'pricking' of musical notation}

Firmly. The reference here is to a swelling erection.

Doted. Pricking, fucking. {Doted echoes 'noted', and puns again on the 'pricking' of musical notation}

Will. Lust.

Wilful. Lecherous.

Eye. Penis. {Also a pun on anus and testicles}

Tired. Fed hungrily on, glutted. {As a bird of prey 'tears' the flesh of its prey}

Queen Elizabeth I sometimes wore gowns with exceptionally low, breast-exposing necklines. A French diplomat meeting the 64-year-old English monarch at court was astonished to 'see the whole of her bosom ['toute sa gorge'], and passing low ... her bosom is somewhat wrinkled, but lower down her flesh is exceedingly white and delicate.' Her 'petticoat of white damask, girdled and open in the front, as was also her chemise, in such a manner that she often opened her dress and one could see all her belly, and even to her navel ... When she raises her head she has a trick of putting both hands on her gown and opening it insomuch as all her belly can be seen.'

In the late 16th and early 17th centuries unmarried virgins wore gowns with very low necklines – however old they were. Another foreign visitor to the court of Queen Elizabeth wrote that her 'bosom was uncovered, as all the English ladies have it till they marry'. There were those who disapproved of the fashion. One commentator railed against the sinful effect bare breasts had on men:

> 'These naked paps [breasts], the devil's gins [traps] and breasts [which these women] embuske up on high, and their round roseate buds immodestly lay forth.'

# *Pertaining to* BALLS

# THE LONELY TESTICLE

## RICHARD III

### Act 1, Scene 1

Shakespeare's Richard III may have a hump for a back, an arm like a 'withered stub', a 'foul lump of deformity' for a body, a 'misshapen Dick' and just one ball, but he certainly knows how to seduce an audience. Shakespeare gives his Machiavellian villain such a distinctively uncomfortable-making charm, that the audience cannot help but fall under his fascinating spell, even though they know him to be a killer who will stop at nothing as he murders his way to the throne.

Here, in the first lines of *Richard III*, he addresses the audience directly in one of the most celebrated soliloquies in Shakespeare. In the hands of a good actor, the speech works like a spell, drawing us into a guilty complicity with his evil plans. By inviting us to dwell on everything that is repulsive about him, he manages to win something approaching our sympathy.

*Richard*  But I, that am not shaped for

sportive tricks . . .

I that am rudely stamped and want love's majesty

To strut before a wanton ambling nymph,

I that am curtailed of this fair proportion . . .
Deformed, unfinished, sent before my time
Into this breathing world scarce half made up –
And that so lamely and unfashionable . . .

*Richard*  But I, whose prick and balls are not properly shaped for sexual tricks. I that am roughly formed and lack an impressive cock to strut before a lusty girl with come-on eyes as she strolls by me soliciting like a whore. I that am castrated and without a proper cock, deformed, unfinished, born premature into this breathing world with only one testicle, and even that one ball so impotent and badly formed.

Shape. Genitals.

Sportive. Sexual.

Wanton. Lascivious.

Ambling. Street-walking like a prostitute.

Curtailed. Cut off at the tail (penis), i.e. castrated.

Proportion. Penis.

Before my time. Born prematurely.

Half made up. Having only a single testicle, being only half a man.

Lamely. Impotently.

Unfashionable. Badly formed.

There is a bawdy anecdote dating from 1601 and frequently repeated in print, concerning Shakespeare and his friend Richard Burbage, the celebrated actor who played Richard III and Hamlet. The two men were co-owners of the theatre company The Lord Chamberlain's Men, which later became The King's Men. Burbage was becoming a huge star with a great female following. The story goes that a groupie invited him to have sex with her, but when he got to her place, he found that someone else had got there first . . .

> 'Upon a time when [Richard] Burbage played Richard III there was a citizen grew so far in liking with him, that before she went from the play she appointed him to come that night unto her by the name of Richard III. Shakespeare, overhearing their conclusion, went before, was entertained at his game ere Burbage came. Then message being brought that Richard III was at the door, Shakespeare caused return to be made that William the Conqueror was before Richard III.'

# ANYONE FOR A KICK IN THE GOOLIES?

## HENRY V

### *Act 1, Scene 2*

In a play about war a whole scene is devoted to a match between two sets of testicles. It's one of the most entertaining scenes in Shakespeare - a French player gives an English player a metaphorical kick in the balls, only to find himself receiving a return hit.

The French ambassador arrives at King Henry's court to warn him against invading France. He comes with an unusual present from the Dauphin. The punning subtext throughout relates to the insult represented by his gift – the message from the Dauphin is that Henry doesn't have the balls for war.

> *Ambassador*  You cannot revel into dukedoms there
> {in France}.
> {The Dauphin} therefore sends you, meeter for
> your spirit,
> This tun of treasure ...
> *King Harry*  What treasure, uncle?

*Exeter* {*opening the tun*} Tennis balls, my liege.

*King Harry* We are glad the Dauphin is so pleasant
with us.

His present and your pains we thank you for.

When we have matched our rackets to these balls,

We will in France, by God's grace, play a set

Shall strike his father's crown into the hazard.

*Ambassador* You cannot play around in the French

kingdoms and think you can conquer them. The

Dauphin therefore sends you, more fittingly, for

your puny prick and impotent spunk, this cask

of potent semen.

*King Harry* What kind of semen is it, uncle?

*Exeter* The stuff of whore-house balls, my lord.

*King Harry* We are glad the Dauphin is so facetious

with us. We thank you for his balls and your cock.

When we have matched our pricks to these balls,

we will in France, by God's grace, play a set that

will strike his father's cock into his arse.

Spirit. Prick, spunk.

Tun. Barrel.

Treasure. Potent semen.

Tennis. Whore-house. {A play of the time has the line: 'the stews {whorehouses} had wont to be the tennis-court'}

Pains. Cock. {Sounds like 'penis'}

Rackets. Pricks.

Crown. Cock. {A 'crown' is circular. The word was also used for vagina and rump}

Hazard. Arse. {'The hazard' is a reference to the aperture in the back wall of an Elizabethan tennis court}

# A TRAGIC TALE OF MISTAKEN IDENTITY

## A MIDSUMMER NIGHT'S DREAM

### Act 5, Scene 1

An amateur drama group puts on a play for a royal audience. But it is a play in which the characters kiss testicles and tangled pubic hair, and a lover has trouble locating his girlfriend's vagina.

In what is arguably the funniest scene in all Shakespeare, Bottom the weaver and his fellow craftsmen put on a show for the Duke and his courtiers. The play is the same plot as that of the tragedy, *Romeo and Juliet*, so they call it – quite appropriately, as it turns out – 'A tedious, brief scene of young Pyramus and his love Thisbe: very tragical mirth.'

*Thisbe* My cherry lips have often kissed thy stones,

Thy stones with lime and hair knit up in thee . . .

*Pyramus* O kiss me through the hole of this vile wall.

*Thisbe* I kiss the wall's hole, not your lips at all.

*Thisbe*  My vaginal lips have often kissed your
balls, your bollocks that are tangled up with slime
and hair together.

*Pyramus*  O fuck me through the hole of this
shaggy wall.

*Thisbe*  I kiss the arse hole between your buttocks,
not your genitals at all.

Cherry lips. The reference is to
vaginal lips.
Stones. Testicles, balls.
Lime. Slime.
Kiss. To fuck.

Hole. Arse.
Vile. Shaggy, as of hair.
Wall. Buttocks.
All. Genitals. [Punning on 'awl',
a boring-tool]

# *Pertaining to*
# PUBES

# ARTIFICIAL RUGS

## HENRY V

### Act 3, Scene 7

Bestiality, sodomy and false pubic hair are the topics under review in the French camp on the eve of the Battle of Agincourt. Like the English, the French are waiting impatiently for dawn and for the fighting to begin, and they start squabbling among themselves.

The French courtiers discuss the attributes of their horses (their whores) and embark on a slanging-match in which they insult each other's sexual habits. Allusions to bestiality lurk just below the surface of the dialogue, and the relentless wordplay on 'horses' and 'whores' so confuses the matter of gender, that the Duke of Bourbon ends up saying: 'My mistress wears *his* own hair.'

Here, Bourbon has just boasted that he has composed a sonnet to his horse, because 'my horse is my mistress'.

*Orléans*  Your mistress bears well . . .

*Constable*  Mine was not bridled.

*Bourbon*  O then belike she was old and gentle, and you rode like a kern of Ireland, your French hose off, and in your strait strossers.

*Constable*  You have good judgement in horsemanship.

*Bourbon* Be warned by me then: they that ride so, and ride not warily, fall into foul bogs. I had rather have my horse to my mistress.

*Constable* I had as lief have my mistress a jade.

*Bourbon* I tell thee, Constable, my mistress wears his own hair.

*Orléans* Your mistress bears you like a whore.

*Constable* Mine wasn't bridled. I didn't put my cock in her mouth.

*Bourbon* Then it's likely she was an old whore and not feeling lusty.

It sounds like you rode her like a bare-arsed soldier of Ireland, without your French baggy breeches, and instead wore your tight-round-the-arse trousers, with no codpiece covering your cock.

*Constable* You have exceedingly good knowledge of what makes a good whore.

*Bourbon* Be careful: they that ride like that, ride wearing nothing, fall into the filthy buttocks of a whore. I'd rather have my horse as my whore.

**Constable** I'd rather my mistress be a worn-out, syphilitic whore with thin hair.

**Bourbon** I tell you, Constable, my whore hasn't got the clap – he has no need of a false bush of pubic hair.

Horse. Whore.

Bear. To bear the weight of a lover during sex.

Well. Whore, vagina. {A 'well' receives liquid}

Mine was not bridled. Mine did not have the bridle-bit in her mouth, i.e. she did not have my cock in her mouth.

Old. Whore. {Sounds like 'hold', as in 'does she hold well?'}

Gentle. Not lusty.

Kern of Ireland. Light-armed (and light-clad) Irish foot-soldier. Kerns famously wore no breeches, like the Scottish Highlanders.

French hose. Loose, baggy trousers.

Strait strossers. Tight trousers resembling tights and with no codpiece.

Horsemanship. Extensive knowledge of whores.

Not warily. Wearing nothing.

Foul. Filthy.

Bogs. Whores, buttocks.

Jade. Worn-out whore, whose hair is thin from the effects of syphilis.

Wears his own hair. Has no need of a *merkin*, a false wig for a bald female pudendum.

# EXPLORING THE UNDERGROWTH
## VENUS AND ADONIS
### *Lines 235–238*

Shakespeare's goddess Venus is reduced to a beast in heat in one of the sexiest poems in English literature. She is in a permanent state of erotic arousal – and sexual frustration. Adonis, the young teenage boy she is frantically trying to seduce, is a prude, completely resistant to her voluptuous body which is continuously and literally oozing with sexual desire.

She does not lack, she tells him, 'juice'. She can't understand how any male could turn down the offer of so enticing a female body. 'My flesh is soft and plump, my marrow [clitoris] burning.' And Venus is enormous compared to Adonis – he's forever being crushed under the weight of the huge expanse of her bosom, and struggling to come up for air.

Embracing the reluctant boy, Venus invites him to 'feed' and 'graze' on the landscape of her sexual parts, her swelling pudenda and her pubic hair.

'Within this limit is relief enough,

Sweet bottom-grass, and high delightful plain,

Round rising hillocks, brakes obscure and rough,

To shelter thee from tempest and from rain ...'

'Within this pasture you'll find plenty of sexual gratification, sweet-tasting pubic hair, and a high delightful vulva, round, swelling buttocks, with pubes dark and shaggy, to shelter you from tempest and from rain.'

| | |
|---|---|
| Relief. Sexual gratification. | Rising. Swelling. |
| Sweet. Sweet-tasting. | Hillocks. Buttocks. |
| Bottom-grass. Pubic hair. | Brakes. Pubes. |
| Plain. Vulva. | Rough. Shaggy. |

Venus's frustration – and the comic force of the poem – reaches its height when she pulls Adonis on top of her and thinks, at last, he's going to do it: 'Now is she in the very lists of love [ecstasy of desire], / Her champion mounted for the hot encounter'. But so, coition is to be denied her yet again. Her thirst for him now is unbearable: 'He will not manage [fuck] her, although he mount her.' (595–598)

# AN EXCELLENT HEAD OF HAIR

## TWELFTH NIGHT

### *Act 1, Scene 3*

Sir Andrew Aguecheek ('pox infested buttocks') and Sir Toby Belch ('fart'), are drinking themselves under the table as usual. The Countess Olivia's gentlewoman, Maria, is serving up obscene sexual puns as well as beer.

The witless Sir Andrew, who lacks a brain as well as balls, has some trouble reading the sexual subtext, but he still unwittingly produces a range of filthy doubles entendres (rather like Mistress Quickly in *Henry IV*, see page 147). The result, as here, is that his conversation doesn't make much sense.

Here, Sir Toby mocks Sir Andrew for his 'excellent head of hair'.

*Sir Andrew*  I'll ride home tomorrow, Sir Toby.

*Sir Toby*  Pourquoi ... ?

*Sir Andrew*  What is 'Pourquoi'? Do, or not do? I would I had bestowed that time in the tongues that I have in fencing, dancing, and bear-baiting. O, had I but followed the arts!

*Sir Toby*  Then hadst thou had an excellent head of hair.

*Sir Andrew* But it becomes me well enough, does't not?

*Sir Toby* Excellent, it hangs like flax on a distaff, and I hope to see a housewife take thee between her legs and spin it off.

*Sir Andrew* I'll get my end away tomorrow, Sir Toby.

*Sir Toby* Pourquoi?

*Sir Andrew* What is 'Pourquoi'? To fuck, or not to fuck? I wish I'd spent as much of my spunk in the clitorises of women as I have in thrusting, fucking, and bearing the weight in the sex-act. O cunt, if only I'd followed my arse!

*Sir Toby* You used to have an excellent lewd arse, prick-head and pubic hair then.

*Sir Andrew* The pubic hair becomes me well enough, don't you think?

*Sir Toby* Lewdly excellent, it hangs like the hairs round a prick, and I hope to see a whore take you between her legs and jerk you off.

Ride home. To get one's end away, mount someone sexually and thrust home.

Do, or not do? To fuck or not to fuck?

Bestowed time. Discharged semen.

Tongues. Clitorises.

Fencing. Thrusting sexually.

Dancing. Fucking.

Bear-baiting. Bearing the weight of a partner during sex.

O. Cunt. {Words for circular and ring shapes often denote the vagina}

Arts. Arse.

Excellent. Arse, lewd. {From the Latin *excellere* meaning 'to rise up', 'to surpass', 'to be eminent'; often referring to the anus or buttocks}

Head. The head of the prick.

Flax. Pubic hair. {In spinning, flax hung in long, thin, yellowish strings on a pole held between the knees}

Housewife. Whore.

Distaff. Prick.

Spin it off. To jerk off.

The colour yellow was traditionally associated with men who couldn't get it up, and also with shit and fart-smells. It also had associations with effeminacy. In Shakespeare's time an effeminate male was not seen as homosexual, but as weak and impotent, and over-influenced by women. A description of an 'effeminate' man in Shakespeare's day described him as 'a woman's man' who kept a mistress. The clichéd image of effeminacy which we often tend to associate with homosexuals today did not arise until the 18th century.

*Pertaining to*

# IMPOTENCE

———————————————

———————————————

# FIFTEEN WAYS TO TELL A MAN HE'S FUCKING USELESS

## THE COMEDY OF ERRORS

*Act 4, Scene 2*

Faced with the knowledge that her husband Antipholus of Ephesus has not only been unfaithful to her with a whore, but has also come on to her sister Luciana, Adriana deals with her pain by listing his sexual inadequacies.

The comedy of the scene comes from the audience knowing that it's not Adriana's husband who has tried to seduce Luciana, but his twin brother, Antipholus of Syracuse.

*Adriana* He is deformèd, crookèd, old, and sere,

Ill-faced, worse-bodied, shapeless everywhere,

Vicious, ungentle, foolish, blunt, unkind,

Stigmatical in making, worse in mind.

*Adriana*  He can't get it up. He's got a small dick. He's got no spunk in his balls – he's like a clapped-out whore. He's got an ugly, unmanly arse, and the cock and bollocks of a pimp – his whole lunchbox is a dog's breakfast in every way.

He's sexually defective, violent, dips his dick in all over town, though being castrated, his pork sword's short of a prick, he's impotent, a wanker, and he fucks like a deformed beast, thinking of whores.

Deformèd. Having a small cock.
Crookèd. Impotent.
Old. Whore. {'Hold' as in 'hold a hand', a pun on holding a cock, with the 'h' dropped}
Sere. Dry, withered.
Ill. Unmanly, ugly.
Worse. Pimp. {Sounds like 'whores', and by extension means pimp}
Body. Genitals.
Shapeless. The suggestion is of deformed genitalia.

Vicious. Sexually defective.
Foolish. Promiscuous.
Blunt. Cut short, impotent.
Unkind. Wanker. {'Unkind' means unnatural, as is masturbation since it is sex without procreation}
Stigmatical. Born with defective genitals.
Making. Having sex, fucking.
Worse in mind. Thinking of whores. {'Worse' sounds like 'whores'}

The word 'stigmatical' was also used to describe the London prostitutes who had been branded on the forehead with an 'R' for Rogue under the terms of a decree of James I. This seemed a gentle punishment compared with the one proposed in Oliver Cromwell's Act of 1650 that they should be

> *'cauterised and seared with a hot iron on the cheek, forehead or some other part of their body that might be seen, to the end that the honest and chaste Christians might be discerned from the adulterous children of Satan.'*

# BALL-BREAKERS

## KING LEAR

### Act 2, Scene 4

King Lear's two noxious daughters really know how to break a man's balls. He's given away his kingdom to them, and their response is to make him get rid of all his knights. For Lear, his men represent the only vestige of power, manhood and self-respect remaining to him. By depriving him of them, his daughters metaphorically castrate him.

Lear will be reduced to going down on his knees to beg his own daughter to let him stay in her house. But as the storm begins to rage outside, she orders the gates to be locked against him. The King of Britain, thrust out into the violent elements, becomes just another of the nation's homeless.

Lear's Fool, who is the wise man of the play, constantly warns the King that his daughters will deprive him of his manhood. Here, the Fool describes Lear's psychological state with his customary ribald, but always discerning, riddling, describing his impotent testicles as a torn scrotum.

*Fool* Fathers that wear rags

  Do make their children blind;

But fathers that bear bags

  Shall see their children kind.

Fortune, that arrant whore,

  Ne'er turns the key to the poor.

*Fool* Fathers who are robbed of their balls and left with a ragged scrotum make their children blind to their needs. But fathers who have their testicles intact, will have children who are kind to them.

Fortune, that out-and-out whore, never opens the door to the impotent.

Rags. A torn or castrated scrotum, suggesting impotence. {'Rags' also refers to fragments of hard rough 'stone', or fragments of 'testicle'}
Bags. Scrota, i.e. plural of 'scrotum'. {The reference is to fathers who have kept their scrotum intact, and are therefore sexually potent}

Turns the key. i.e. opens the door. {The Fool is suggesting that Lear's daughters have closed their doors to him and his men now that he is penniless (i.e. without a penis and testicles). Like whores, they won't open the door to punters who can't pay, or are impotent}
Poor. Impotent.

*King Lear* ends with a stage strewn with corpses. *Hamlet, Othello* and *Macbeth* leave us with the same tragic scenario. It is almost impossible to imagine being in the audience at the theatre, stunned and drained by the tragedy you have just witnessed, to be then entertained by a clown or group of clowns singing filthy songs, dancing and leaping about, making rude gestures to match the bawdy words and making you laugh till you cried. But that is what audiences were given even at the end of tragedies.

After watching Lear cradling his daughter and asking his heart to break, a rhyming farce would follow – often about a housewife caught by her husband having sex with her lover.

The clown in Shakespeare's company was Will Kemp, who played Falstaff in the two parts of *Henry IV* and Bottom in *A Midsummer Night's Dream*. His coarse, obscene jigs were so popular that everyone sang them as they worked and walked down the street: 'whores, beadles, bawds, sergeants all filthily chant Kemp's jig'.

# Pertaining to
# VIRGINITY

# A HORRIFIC DEFLOWERING

## TITUS ANDRONICUS

### Act 2, Scene 3

Gang rape and gruesome mutilation, beheadings, human sacrifice, butchery and cannibalistic feasting. Shakespeare's first tragedy was a ghoulish blood-bath, in which revenge comes in the form of the avenger dressed up as a chef serving an evil mother her sons baked in a pie. This is Shakespeare's horror play, with more than twelve violent deaths. But if this sounds more like a grisly farce than tragedy, the play in performance is far from funny.

The most disturbing of all acts of violence in Shakespeare is the rape of Lavinia in *Titus Andronicus*. The gruesome act takes place offstage, but the prelude and aftermath leave us in no doubt of its horrific nature.

Lavinia will come on stage (2.4), blood pouring from the two stumps where her hands have been chopped off, and blood seeping through her lips from where her tongue has been cut out. Her helpless family – and the audience – look on in appalled disbelief.

Her rapists will ensure their victim will be unable to tell anyone what they have done. But Lavinia's uncle will place a pole in her mouth for her to 'write' down what has happened and she is forced to re-live – and the audience to imagine – the unspeakable acts she has been made to perform with her hands and tongue.

Her rapists, Demetrius and Chiron, urged by their mother, Tamora, Queen of the Goths, have murdered Lavinia's betrothed, Bassianus, before her eyes, and intend to 'make his dead trunk a pillow' on which to rape and butcher her. Their mother tells them to do the job properly.

*Lavinia* 'Tis present death I beg, and one thing more

That womanhood denies my tongue to tell.

O, keep me from their worse-than-killing lust,

And tumble me into some loathsome pit . . .

*Tamora* So should I rob my sweet sons of their fee.

No, let them satisfy their lust on thee . . .

*Lavinia* No grace, no womanhood – ah, beastly

  creature,

The blot and enemy to our general name,

Confusion fall –

*Chiron* Nay then, I'll stop your mouth.

   *{The sons throw Bassianus' body in the pit and drag*

     *Lavinia away}*

*Tamora* Farewell, my sons. See that you make her sure . . .

And let my spleenful sons this trull deflower.

*Lavinia* It is immediate death I beg, and one other

thing that my chaste modesty forbids my tongue to say.

O, keep me from their worse-than-killing lust, and

tumble me into some loathsome pit.

*Tamora* What, and I deprive my sons of the sexual

pleasure that's their right? No, let them satisfy their lust on you.

*Lavinia* You have no gentleness! No womanly feelings! You whore that mates with animals, you're no woman. You're the stain on womanhood, an enemy to the reputation of women. Let destruction fall –

*Chiron* Nay, then, I'll stop your mouth.

*{The sons throw Bassianus' body in the pit and drag Lavinia away}*

*Tamora* Farewell my sons. See that you treat her like a whore. Let my spunk-filled sons deflower this filthy slut.

| | |
|---|---|
| Beastly. Bestial in a sexual sense. | a whore. |
| Creature. Whore. | Spleenful. Full of spunk. |
| Make her sure. i.e. treat her like | Trull. Filthy slut. |

The blood and gore of *Titus Andronicus* may strike us as excessive or farcical, but for Shakespeare's audience, such grisly spectacles were part of everyday life. Punishment in his day was made ghoulishly public, mainly because the enforcement of law was so difficult, but also, in the case of political prisoners, because the public needed to be discouraged from taking part in rebellion against the state. In Queen Elizabeth I's time there was no proper police force, only a few constables to keep law and order.

If you lived in London you could witness the sickening sight of prisoners being hanged, drawn and quartered. Traitors were strung up till they were half-dead, their bodies chopped into quarters, their bowels ripped out and their limbs cut off, and their flesh tossed into a vat of boiling water.

# NO SEX BEFORE MARRIAGE

## THE TEMPEST

### Act 4, Scene 1

Shakespeare may have been the original English toy-boy. He was only 18 years old when he married Anne Hathaway. She was 26 years old. And she was more than three months pregnant.

Eighteen was considered a young age for a man to marry at that time (the average age was 28), and women were usually at least two years younger than their husbands.

It's tempting to imagine Will being fascinated by this older woman. Anne Hathaway certainly didn't conform to society's ideal of a maidenly bride on the threshold of womanhood. Both her parents were dead, she was financially independent and free to choose her own husband and to do pretty much as she pleased. Perhaps Anne's unusual degree of freedom and independence provided Shakespeare with the inspiration for his strong and independent-minded heroines.

In *The Tempest* a daughter's virginity is shown to be a valuable commodity, a part of a father's dream of dynasty. Here, Prospero warns his daughter's suitor that if he has sex with her before they are married, the union will be barren and they will end up hating each other.

*Prospero*  Take my daughter. But

If thou dost break her virgin-knot before

All sanctimonious ceremonies may

With full and holy rite be ministered,

No sweet aspersion shall the heavens let fall

To make this contract grow; but barren hate,

Sour-eyed disdain, and discord, shall bestrew

The union of your bed with weeds so loathly

That you shall hate it both.

*Prospero*  Take my daughter, but if you break her
virginal membrane before all sacred ceremonies are
carried out with full and holy ritual, no sweet-tasting
showers of semen shall the heavens let fall to make this
marriage grow. Barren hate, cruel-eyed disdain and
discord shall be strewn on the union of your semen with
weeds so abhorrent that you shall both ending up hating
to have sex.

| | |
|---|---|
| Virgin-knot. Vaginal membrane. Sweet aspersions. Showers of semen. | Bed. Seed-bed. {The image is of a marriage bed covered in seed or semen, to breed children} |

Among the rumours surrounding Elizabeth I's sex life was one that she was indeed a Virgin Queen. Ben Jonson, playwright and friend of Shakespeare, said that she had a membrane on her so thick that no man could penetrate her, 'though for her delight she tried many'. Jonson related the story, which was published in *Conversations with Drummond* (1618–19), of a French Monsieur who decided to have a go at cutting it, but she was too frightened of the pain and he was too frightened of her sentencing him to death if he caused her pain.

Shakespeare's three brothers never married. He seems to have been very close to Joan (the only one of his three sisters to survive childhood), who married very late, at the age of 30, and named her first child after his godfather, Will. Shakespeare's eldest daughter Susanna married at the same age her mother did – at 26.

# COLLATERAL DAMAGE

## HENRY V

### Act 3, Scene 3

The human cost of war is a central theme of virtually every one of Shakespeare's history plays, and his many depictions of the horrors of military conflict show particular revulsion for the acts of rape carried out by soldiers.

Here, as Henry V threatens to attack Harfleur, he addresses the governor of the French town with a terrifyingly graphic image of what his soldiers will do if the town won't surrender to him.

*King Harry* The gates of mercy shall be all shut up,

And the fleshed soldier, rough and hard of heart,

In liberty of bloody hand shall range

With conscience wide as hell, mowing like grass

Your fresh fair virgins and your flow'ring infants . . .

What is't to me . . .

If your pure maidens fall into the hand

Of hot and forcing violation? . . .

. . . why, in a moment, look to see
The blind and bloody soldier with foul hand
Defile the locks of your shrill-shrieking daughters.

*King Harry*  The gates of mercy shall be all locked up, and the sexually inflamed soldiers, rough, and with stiffened pricks, will have the freedom to shed spunk with their penises. And with a clear conscience range as wide as hell, mowing like grass your fresh fair virgins and your budding infants. What is it to me if your pure maidens are forced to yield to the pricks of hot and violent violation? In a moment, look to see the blind and spunk-filled soldier with his foul cock defile the maidenheads of your daughters, making them shriek with horror.

Fleshed. Sexually inflamed.
Hard. Erect.
Bloody. Spunk-filled.
Hand. Prick. {Hand as a phallic symbol, and also suggesting 'holding' as in holding the 'hand' in masturbation}
Defile the locks. Punning on the virginal membrane 'locked' against defilement.

*Henry V* is always topical because it examines the question: Can there ever be such a thing as a 'just war'?

For the play's original audience, the Battle of Agincourt (1415) was recent history, celebrated as a resounding English triumph over the French. So it is even more remarkable for a playwright to have included a scene in which the audience was encouraged to question the morality of this war. The scene comes at the beginning of the fourth act, at a point in the drama when the audience would have been anticipating speeches of patriotic zeal on the part of the soldiers.

It is the eve of battle. An ordinary soldier, Michael Williams, is profoundly troubled that Henry's war against France is unethical. He worries that if it isn't morally just, there will be a terrible human cost to pay for 'all those legs and arms and heads, chopped off in battle'. When Henry, in disguise, says the king's cause is 'just', and the war 'honourable', Shakespeare gives Williams five words to say in reply – words which have echoed down the centuries, and never more chillingly apposite than today: 'That's more than we know.'

*Pertaining to*

# PIMPS

# A SLEEPLESS NIGHT FOR TROILUS'S PRICK

## TROILUS AND CRESSIDA

### *Act 4, Scene 2*

A pimp addresses a man's cock and asks it how it got on last night with the vagina of his niece, Cressida.

Shakespeare's Cressida is an unfaithful slag or she's a helpless victim of male aggression and power politics. She has usually been characterised as the first (mostly by male critics and directors). But the play makes her much more interesting than either of these. She's a complex mix of sexual desire, low self-esteem, fear of being betrayed by men, and relying on others to define her self-identity.

Cressida's uncle, Pandarus, whose name means 'pimp', has arranged a night of sex for her with the man she loves, Troilus. Cressida's first words to him are: 'Will you walk in, my lord?' which sounds like a whore at the door of a brothel soliciting. The following morning, Pandarus arrives to see how they've got on in bed.

*Pandarus* How now, how now, how go maidenheads?
*{To Cressida}* Here, you, maid! Where's my cousin
Cressid?

*Cressida {Unveiling}* Go hang yourself. You naughty,
mocking uncle!
You bring me to do - and then you flout me too.

*Pandarus* To do what? To do what? - Let her say what. -
What have I brought you to do? . . .

    *{Turns to address Troilus's prick}*

*Pandarus* Ha ha! Alas, poor wretch. Ah, poor *capocchia*,
hast not slept tonight? *{To Cressida}* Would he not - a
naughty man - let it sleep? . . .

*Cressida {To Troilus}* Did not I tell you? Would he were
knocked i'th'head.

*Pandarus* Well, well, now, what's the price of virgin
membranes?

*{To Cressida}* Here you, (no longer) virgin - where's my
cousin Cressid?

*Cressida {Unveiling}* Go hang yourself by the balls. You
wicked, mocking uncle! You bring me here me to have
sex - and then you scoff at me, too.

*Pandarus* To do what? To fuck what? - let her tell us

what – What have I brought you to fuck?

{*Turns to address Troilus's prick*}

*Pandarus* Ha, ha! Oh you poor wretch. Ah, poor prick-head, haven't you slept tonight? {*To Cressida*} Would he not – this wicked cock – let Troilus sleep?

*Cressida* {*To Troilus*} Didn't I tell you? I wish the tip of his prick was given a knocking.

Hang. i.e. hanging balls.

To do. To fuck.

*Capocchia*. Penis tip, foreskin.

Head. Tip of the penis.

# UNWANTED PURCHASE

## MEASURE FOR MEASURE

### Act 1, Scene 2

A pimp and brothel madam are shown to have a higher sense of morality than a Puritan in this play. The deputy ruler, Angelo, a man so coldly chaste 'that when he makes water his urine is congealed ice', is Shakespeare's most disturbing moral hypocrite. He promises to reprieve the sentence of execution of a novice nun's innocent brother if she has sex with him, but he has every intention of having the man's head cut off once she has succumbed to him.

The ruler of the state, the Duke, is too cowardly to enforce the resurrected law against sex before marriage, and creeps around the city disguised as a friar dispensing clerical advice he has no moral right to do. In this society, judicial murder of young people for having sex is legal, but if you're a ruler of the state you can get away with it. Sex for sale is illegal. The law, in this play, is an ass.

The scenes in the whorehouse provide comic relief from the play's dark elements, and offer the most realistic portrayal of life in the brothels in Shakespeare. The madam, Mistress Overdone (Mistress 'Overfucked'), is here the butt of her customers' obscene jokes.

*Lucio* Behold, behold, where Madam Mitigation comes! I have purchased as many diseases under her roof as come to - ...

*Second Gentleman* To three thousand dolours a year?

*First Gentleman* Ay, and more.

*Lucio* A French crown more.

*First Gentleman* Thou art always figuring diseases in me, but thou art full of error - I am sound.

*Lucio* Nay not, as one would say, healthy, but so sound as things that are hollow - thy bones are hollow, impiety has made a feast of thee.

*First Gentleman* {*To Mistress Overdone*} How now, which of your hips has the most profound sciatica?

*Lucio* Look, look, where Madam Who-relieves-all-sexual desire, will reach orgasm! I have purchased as many venereal diseases from her whores and their cunts, under this brothel madam's roof as come to -

*Second Gentleman* To three thousand dollars worth of diseases and pain a year?

*First Gentleman* Yes and one more.

*Lucio* A French syphilitic boil more.

*First Gentleman*  You're always imagining I've got syphilis, but you're completely wrong - I'm sound in health.

*Lucio*  No not, as you would say, sound in health, but you make sounds in the way that hollow bones sound. You've got the bone-ache - bones that have been made brittle by VD.

*First Gentleman*  {*To Mistress Overdone*} How now, which of your hips has the most profound venereal sciatica?

Madam. Female pimp, brothel keeper.

Mitigation. Mistress Overdone is so called because she relieves sexual desire.

Comes. Reaches orgasm.

Roof. Cunt, whore, pubes. {Punning on 'ruff' because of its circular shape; on 'ruffa' meaning whore; and on 'roofs' meaning heads, and by extension bald heads - hair loss being a symptom of syphilis}

Dolours. Diseases. {Punning on 'dollars' in the monetary sense}

French crown. Baldness caused by syphilis. {Syphilis was sometimes known as the 'French disease', see page 230}

Hollow bones. Syphilis. {The reference is to 'bone-ache', a term for syphilis. The disease was also known as 'Neapolitan bone-ache', see page 230}

The first performance of *Measure for Measure* we know about is one performed for King James I at the Banqueting Hall in Whitehall on 26 December 1604. Shakespeare's company, previously called The Lord Chamberlain's Men, was given royal status when James ascended the throne, and thus became The King's Men.

What must the king, a known homosexual, have made of the line spoken by the brothel customer Lucio, when he remarks (3.2) that the Duke of Vienna is not inclined to have sex with women? 'I have never heard the absent Duke much detected for women; he was not inclined that way.'

# APPENDIX

# APPENDIX

This is not an exhaustive list, but enough to demonstrate the fertility of Shakespeare's sexual vocabulary.

## PUN WORDS ON FEMALE GENITALS

affairs, all, another thing, awl

baldrick, belly, bird's nest, blackness, bogs, bottle, bond of chastity, bosom, box unseen, breach, buckles, bud

case, catch, charged chambers, cherry, cheveril, circle, city, clack-dish, cliff, commodity, con-, conscience, constable, contrary, corner, coun-, countenance, country, crown, crack, cunning, cut

dale, dearest bodily part, den, dewlap, dial, dice, door

ear, eyes

face, fair parts, fan, favours, field, forest, flower, forfended place

garden, gate, gift, glass, gown, grace

head, hell, hole, hook, home

jewel

key, knock

lap, land, leather, ling, lip, load, loins, low countries

maidenhead, mark, matter, medlar, modest, mouldy

nest of spicery, nature/natural, nether, Netherlands, nick, nony, nothing/noting

O, open-arse, orchard, organs of increase

paradise, park, passage, peace, piece, pit, Pillicock-hill, pink, place, placket, plum, plum-tree, pond, poop, presents, private, pudency, purpose

quaint/acquaint, quick, quiver

re, roof, rose, rudder, ruff, rural

sake, salmon's tail, score, scorn, scrubbed, scut, secret parts, secret things, shape, share, shore, side, snatch, Spain, sweet

tail, tale, tawny, thigh, thing, token, tongue, treasure/treasury, true

velvet, velvet leaves, Venus' glove, vice, voice

well, wings, what, white, will, wit, withered pear, word, wound

## PUN WORDS ON MALE GENITALS

acorn, all, answer, apples, awl

bear, baggage, bags, bawl, billiards, bolt, boult, bowels, bowls, brag, bugle, bullets

caius, *capocchia*, card, carrot, catch, cheveril, chin, circle, coat, cock, cods, cod heads, codpiece, compass, con, conjure it down, crown, curse, curst

damsons, dance, dance with one's heels, dart, dewlap, discard, distaff, draw up, due, dulcet

ears, eat, edge, eel, eleven, end, engine, enlargement, erection, exceed, exchange flesh, eyes

fall backwards, feather, fistula, flesh, foot, fork

gift, grace, gracious

hand, hang, head, hogshead, holy-thistle, hood, hook, horn, hose

inch, index, inside lip, instrument

jet, jewel

kicky-wicky, knock

lag-end, lance, leek, lightning, little finger, little witnesses, loins

malice

natural, needle, neither, nether, noon, nose, note, nothing, nuts

oats, oaths, occasion, organ

pains, pair, passage, pen, piece, pike, Pillicock, pin, pinch, pink, pistol, pizzle, bull's pizzle, place, plums, poll-axe, pear, post, potato-finger, potent, presence, present, private, proportion, pudding, purpose, purse

quick

R, rags, raise, re, resolution, ring, Roger, root

sake, sceptre, score, shame, shape, share, shin, short, size, skin, spirit, spleen, spur, spurn, stake, stalk, stand, stand to (it), standard, stiff, sting, stump, sweet, sword

taper, tender, thing, high, thorn, three, three-inch fool, title, token,

tongue, tool, torch, train, true, twelve, twain, twin, twist

vice, voice

weapon, well, will, wine, wings, whit, white, wit, witness, word, wound, wrong

yard

# PUN WORDS ON SEX

ability, abuse someone's bed, access, accommodate, achieve, acquaint, act, act of shame, act of sport, action, activity, acture, adulterate, adventure, affection, alter, amorous rite, amorously impleacht, angel, angling, angry, answer, appetite, approach, assail, assault attempt

bathe in water, battery, beat, bed, belie, besiege, bestial, bestow, betray, between the sheets, billing, bite, blasted, bliss, blood, blood desire, blow, blow up, blower-up, board, bob, boggler, bolster more than their own, boot, bosom'd, bottle, bout, boy, breach, break, break the pale, bridle, broach, broad awake, budge, bullets, burden, buried with her face upwards, burn out, burn up. burning eye, burthen, business, butcher

call to a reckoning, caper, carnal strings, carry, catching of cold, caterpillar, change the cod's head for the salmon's tail, charge, clap, cleave the pin, climb, clip, cloy, coin, colt, come, come in the rearward of the fashion, come over, come to it, commit, compound, conceive her tale, conflict, contaminated, contend, conversation, convince the honour of, conquer a maiden bed, cope, copesmate, corrupt, couch, cover, crackt within the ring, crop, custom

dally, dance with one's heels, deed of darkness, deed of kind, delight, detested, die, die in a woman's lap, disedge, dishonour, disport, distain, distempered blood, do, do the deed, do one's office, down-bed, downright way, drabbing, draw, draw up, dribbling dart of love, duteous to vices eagerness, ear, easy, eat, edge, effect of love, effusion, eleven, emballing, employ, encounter, enforce, engender, enjoy, enlargement, enraged, enseamèd bed, entice, entreat, errors of the blood, exchange blood, execute

fadings, faint, fall, fall backwards, fall to, favours, feasts of love, feed, feed from home, feel, fig me! finger, fill a bottle with a tun-dish, firk, fire, fit, fit it, flames, flesh one's will, focative, foin, foot, force, forefinger, froth, full-acorned, fountain, foutra, furnished

game, German, gennen, get, get a maidenhead, get into corners, get the sun of, getting-up, giddy, glow, glutton, go, go off, go to it, go to work with, goatish, gracious, graze, groaning, groping for trouts

half-blasted, hand, hand in, hang one's bugle in an invisible baldrick, haec, have, have a hot back, hic, hick, hit, hit it, hit lower, hoc, homage, honeying, horsemanship, hot, hot blood, hot deeds, hot dreams, hot thoughts, hour of love, hunger, husband, husband her bed

incestuous sheets, inclined, indeed, inflamed, insatiate, intend, it, itch

jet, joy, juggle, jump, just

keen, kind, kindle, kiss, kiss with inside lip, knock, knot, know

laughter, lay down, lay it, leap, lend, let in, lie, lie between maids' legs, lie on one's back, lie under, load, loll, lubberly, luxury

make, make a monster, make a son out of one's blood, make defeat of virginity, make holes in a woman's petticoat, make one's heaven in a lady's lap, make one's play, make the beast with two backs, man, manage, mar, meddle with, mell with, mettle, milk, mingle bloods, mirth, momentary trick, mount, mouth, mutual entertainment

nose-painting

occupation, occupy, offend in a dream, one moment's fading mirth, noon, nothing, oil, open

paddling palms, pant, pay, perfect in lying down, performance, piled for a French velvet, pick the lock, pinch, piss one's tallow, pistol-proof, pitch, play on one's back, play the sir, play upon, please oneself on, plough, pluck a sweet, ply, pollute, poop, possess, preposterous, press, pretty, pricking, prick out, pride, prompture of the blood, propt under, pudding, push, put a man in one's belly, put down, put to

quench, quick, quickly, quite

raging motions, raise, raise up, ram, rank, ransack, rate, recompense, relief, rendezvous, rents, reprehend, rest, revel in, revels, revenues, riggish, ripe, rite, roam, rode, rubbing

❧ scale, scratch, secretly open, seduce, serve, service, set to it, set up one's rest, shake, share, shed, sinful fantasy, sing, sink in, sluice, snatch, soil, spin off, spirit, spit, spoil, spot, spread, spurn, stab, stain, stair-work, stamp, stand, stand to, stick, stiff, stint, stir, stomach, stoop, stretch, strike, strive, stuff, stumble, sunburnt, supply the place, surfeit, sully, sweat, sweet, swerve, swinge

❧ take, taste, take down, taking, take off, teem, tempt, thaw, throng, throw, throw down, thrust to the wall,

thump, tick-tack, ticklish, tickle one's catastrophe, tilt with lips, tire on, top, toy in blood, trading, traffic, tread, trick, trim, trot, trunk-work, try, try with finger, tumble, tup, turn i'the bed, turn to, twelve, twist

❧ undermine, understand, undertake, undo, unlace, untrussing, up and down, upshoot, use, usury, utter

❧ vault, virginalling

❧ wag one's tail, wear away, whale to virginity, will, wine, work, wrack, wrestle, wrong

❧ yare, yield one's body to shame

# I N D E X

# INDEX
# OF EXTRACTS

This index lists the Shakespeare plays and poems
from which extracts have been included.